Safe in the Heart of a Miracle

Gloria Teague

Buoy Up
Press

Denton Texas

Cover art by Cindy Robinson MacLellan

Buoy Up Press
An imprint of AWOC.COM Publishing
P.O. Box 2819
Denton, TX 76202

Manufactured in the United States of America

ISBN: 978-1-62016-000-8

Visit the author's website: http://www.gloriateague.com

For Dad, the only father I ever knew:

For teaching me to love a challenge,

For helping me see the value of education,

For never giving me the answers so I had to find them myself, and

For giving me a wooden teddy bear plaque with these words painted on it:

Not flesh of my flesh, Nor bone of my bone, But still miraculously my own.

Never forget for a single minute,

You didn't grow under my heart—but in it.

~ Fleur Conkling Heylinger

Table of Contents

Acknowledgements

My family deserves a big hug for hearing me out, listening to me moan, boosting my morale and ego when it was failing and just for being my all-around loving support. Thank you to the heart of my life: Al, De Anna and Linda.

And Mom, I miss you every day, but never more than when I finish a story, an article or a book. You were always my biggest fan, even when my work was lousy. Thank you for believing in me.

I am blessed with friends who listen to me, who read my blogs, my books, my short stories and who, even when they wanted to scream, kept reminding me I am, indeed, a writer. There are too many to list here but the ones who pushed me the hardest, who listened and validated me, my work, I appreciate all of you. A special thanks to Helen, Cindy, Pat, Libby, Earl, Billy, Beth and Diana. And my deep appreciation to Shirley who loaned me a beautiful mountain cabin when I was down to the wire and needed a quiet place to finish this book. The majority of the words written here were born on Beaver Lake.

I want to thank my publisher, Dan Case, for giving me a chance with the first book and the ones that followed it. I guess I even want to thank him for making me crazy when he'd say, "Gloria, I just checked the stats for this weekend and your book sales are ..." No pressure there!

But most of all, I want to thank God

Almost a Heavenly Day

It was too nice a day to die. It was one of those days that when you walked out your front door, you'd never dream it was your last day on Earth. The birds' song was more melodious, the air smelled sweeter, and the colors were more vivid than on just a regular old workday morning.

David stepped softly behind Theresa, bending his head to kiss the back of her neck as she flipped the eggs in the hot skillet.

"Oh, you better be careful there, lover boy, if you still want your eggs over-easy. Kissing my neck is a sure way to get scrambled eggs."

David leaned around until their noses touched, he grinned at her and said, "You know, Mrs. Green, I never mind getting scrambled up with you." She chuckled as she flipped the dish towel at him, shooing him away. The *snap* it made was loud in the quiet kitchen.

Theresa placed his plate in front of him, then leaned her hip against his shoulder as he sat at the table. She ruffled his hair and he reached up, pushed her hand away. "I have you to know that I worked hard on my hair-do this morning. Now kindly leave me to my supposed eggs over-easy."

Her grin was infectious. "I don't think you're the only Green boy getting into a scrambled mess this morning." David lifted his eyebrows and his grin widened. "Your little brother forgot his anniversary yesterday."

David laughed out loud but lowered it to a chuckle after he saw his wife's expression.

"I'm warning you, David Green, if you ever forget our anniversary ..." He didn't for a minute fall for her faux severity but he went along with the game.

He raised his left hand and crossed his heart. Her face relaxed into a loving smile. "I know you wouldn't honey but, just in case, I'm giving you fair warning now!"

They savored a cup of coffee together before he put on his work shoes and headed out the door.

David held his face up to the sunlight as he walked to the car. He heard his wife, standing in the door behind him, chuckling. "You're going to walk right into a tree, David Green. What are you doing?"

He turned around to grin back at her. "Just thinking it's a great day to be alive."

Arriving right on time at his assigned job location, David was pleasantly surprised to see his younger brother pulling his own work equipment from his truck.

"Hey, how'd I got so lucky to be saddled with my rotten baby brother today?"

Jim's mock sneer didn't fool David. "As you said, just lucky I guess. But it looks like we're both having the same kind of luck today, though. I mean, I'm stuck with a lousy old brother."

"Uh, just older; not old, alright? Okay, my slightly younger brother, we might as well get it over with. The sooner we're done, the sooner we don't have to look at each other." They both laughed; clapped each other on the back and bumped fists.

"Yeah, let's hit it, Dave."

It was an early September morning filled with warmth. The sky was blue, with voluminous ivory clouds drifting lazily overhead. As the men balanced on the hydraulic-powered platform the sun reflected back to them from the dirt-smudged windows they'd been hired to clean. They manipulated the scaffolding higher and higher as the morning wore on. Both of their wives had commented often how fortunate it was they weren't afraid of heights.

In the distance the noon whistle sounded at the foundry down the street. As they frequently did, the brothers sat on the edge of the platform, eating lunch and teasing each other as brothers have a tendency to do.

"I heard you've been singing the white rabbit's song from 'Alice in Wonderland.'"

Jim's brows formed peaks over his eyes. "Huh? I don't remember that one."

David chuckled. "Sure you have. Remember 'I'm late, I'm late, for a very important date?'"

The younger man hung his head then turned to look into his brother's laughing face.

"You're in the doghouse now, huh, Jimbo? Man, your tenth wedding anniversary. How mad is Suze? Though I guess a better question would be: how *long* is she going to be mad?"

"Oh, that is so not funny! Yeah, yeah, I know. That's a big one, alright. Ten years is one that should've been important enough to remember, right? And it's not like she didn't remind me e-v-e-r-y single day, right up to the day before. Maybe I forgot just so I could tune out being reminded so often. Hey, you think she'd buy that?"

"I think you're in for an early freeze and you're going to be wearing your winter coat long before the first snowfall, brother. That house is going to get mighty cold before the forgiving thaw."

"Aw man, you're probably right, David. I'm an idiot. I deserve whatever she throws at me since I'm such a dope."

"Hey, now *that* she might buy!"

"Again, not funny, Dave; not funny at all."

"Aw, sure it is; it's a little funny."

Jim stood up, throwing his apple back into the brown paper sack with such force it punched through the bottom of the bag. Both men leaned over the side of the aluminum railing to watch the apple sail 15 stories toward the ground, barely missing a businessman walking briskly along the sidewalk. As with most people, he was wearing a 21st century accessory, a cell phone at his ear. He was so intent on his conversation he never even noticed the fruited missile that barely missed him. The brothers laughed nervously.

"Whew, way to go, Jim. Compound your bad day by missing an anniversary and knocking a stranger out with an apple."

"Oh, shut up. If you're done stuffing your face, big brother, let's get back to work. I'm ready for this day to end. Come on, let's get our harnesses back on and get these windows done."

It was as both men held the harnesses in their hands, just seconds before they would've been safely tethered, they heard the cable snap. The only thing they had time to do was to look at each other and see the reflection of their own heart-stopping fear.

In horrific memories replayed in future nightmares, it would feel like a bad slap-stick comedy movie done in slow motion, without the canned laughter in the background. Jim was the first to fall and as he went over the edge of the scaffolding, David leapt to save him, making him the last one to go over the edge.

No time, no time, no time.

If anyone could've heard anything, all they would've heard from each brother was, "Please God." People on the ground later said they didn't even hear a scream.

At the age of 34, father of an eight-year-old daughter and a five-year-old son, husband to Suzanne, one day past the tenth anniversary that he'd forgotten, Jim Green was killed on impact.

Two feet away, David Green had landed close enough to stretch one finger and touch his little brother's hand. He tried to speak, to demand Jim talk to him, to assure him that he was alright, to scream at God to make it okay, to tell someone to please! call his beloved Theresa. Then his world faded to black.

His consciousness lifted only briefly while he lay on the grass. He could see a blood-spattered white sheet covering his brother and he wanted to cry, to curse, to plead with the medical personnel racing around.

Please, I'm begging you in the name of all that's holy, just stop everything you're doing, hold on just one minute! Please, don't let him die. Let me go, but save my brother!

The first responder crew was quietly giving orders to each other but was unable to hold back the crowd. From the corner of his eye, David could see the man that had nearly been hit by Jim's apple mere moments before, talking to another man. For a minute, he wished he had been struck deaf in the fall.

"Yeah, I heard the cops talking. That one's alive but he won't make it long. How can anyone fall fifteen floors and still be breathing? It's just a matter of time. I heard they're brothers. This is going to be an awful day for their family. But even if he did live, he'd probably be paralyzed, stuck in a wheelchair the rest of his life, be nothing but a burden. Nah, if I was that guy, I wouldn't want to live."

Even through the mind-numbing fear, the desolation of losing his brother filtered through to his heart. In a flash, he remembered all the times they'd played in their homemade fort, all the times they'd laughed as they teased each other, the time he taught Jim to drive, the time a girl broke his heart in junior high school, the time he stood beside him as his best man. The emotional pain was dominant, blocking all thought. And then the shock began to wear off enough for him to realize the formidable physical assault on his body. He prayed for unconsciousness to escape it all. He wasn't sure he could withstand the pain when it became worse; he didn't think he could survive all of it.

Then he made what would be his last decision for a long, long time. In that moment, David decided to let go and let God. That's when he gave in and slipped away into a coma. In that black trance, his brother was still alive and no pain wracked his own body.

* * *

"Mrs. Green? This is Madison Medical Center. I'm sorry to say this, but there's been an accident involving your husband. Could you please come down here right away?"

"Jim? Something's happened to Jim? What happened?" Her voice rose with each syllable.

"I'm sorry, ma'am—the doctor will explain everything when you get here. Do you need someone to bring you?"

"No, I don't need a ride! I need to know what happened to my husband ... now!"

"Mrs. Green, if you'll please calm down ..."

Suzanne Green slammed the phone down and reached for her car keys. On the way to the hospital she called her mother. Though she was sobbing, she managed to get out the words to ask her mother to pick up the kids at school, tell them only that their father had gotten hurt, and take care of them until she called her back.

Her sister-in-law was the first person she saw who she knew when she ran into the ER. Theresa was kneeling on the floor, sobbing uncontrollably. When she saw Suzanne, she jumped up to run to her, nearly knocking her down with her embrace.

"Theresa, what happened? Where are the guys? What's going on? Please, please, honey, slow down. I can't understand what you're saying."

"The cable ... the platform ... they fell."

"They fell while they were working? How far up were they? Theresa, answer me!"

"Fif ... fifteen floors."

"Oh, dear God! Are they okay? Are they hurt?"

These words caused Theresa to again sink to the floor, sobbing. The only word Suzanne could make out was *dead*. She grabbed the other woman's shoulders and pulled her up from the floor and held her.

"Oh, honey, I'm so sorry. Oh, God, I'm so sorry about David. What can I do? Can I call someone?"

Theresa shook her head and she closed her eyes. When she opened them she took a deep breath, her words caught on the next sob. "Not David, Suzanne. It's Jim."

It took several seconds for the words to register, to fully impact her heart. Suzanne fell against the olive-colored wall and slid to the floor, moaning "Noooooooooooooo." Nurses knelt beside both women, trying, in vain, to comfort them. Suzanne became so distraught she had to be taken to a separate room for a doctor to explain what had happened to Jim, the man who she had given the cold shoulder just this morning. And for what? A lousy anniversary—the last one they'd ever share.

The physician's voice was firm, yet kind. "Theresa, let's get you off the floor. Come on, go with me to my office here around the corner. We need to talk about your husband."

She rose quickly to her feet; staying right on the doctor's heels as he walked down the hallway. She managed to pull herself together so she could listen and ask coherent questions.

The moment the office door closed, "Is he dead?" The doctor motioned for her to sit down but she shook her head.

"Mrs. Green, this is going to be a long conversation so I'm asking you to take a seat. No, your husband is not dead."

Theresa dropped to the plush leather chair at the corner of his desk. "How bad is he?"

Dr. Thomas hung his lab coat on a hook before he sat down behind his desk. "He's not good. I won't lie to you; it's bad. It's very bad."

"Okay, I'm settled down now. I can take it. Tell me everything."

He looked at her closely, sternly, "I need to have you stay with me here. You need to make decisions that may affect whether or not your husband lives or dies."

Her eyes filled with fresh tears and she gasped, but she quickly regained control.

"Tell me."

He folded his hands on top of his desk and cleared his throat. "First of all, his internal injuries were so traumatic, I had to open him up in the emergency room. I couldn't take a chance on taking him to OR because I didn't think he'd make it that far. We've stabilized him to the point that he can now be taken upstairs to start surgery, if you consent. Know ahead of time, it's going to be a long, arduous ordeal.

You're going to feel as if you've been part of a marathon that lasts for days, weeks."

"If I consent? Of course I will. Why wouldn't I?"

"Let me give you an idea of what David is facing and this is just today. Remember that a patient's condition can turn on a dime, at any moment."

She nodded in understanding, as much as she could at the moment.

"If he even makes it to surgery, and survives the many operations that are necessary, he'll be in rehab for months afterward. All of this depends on whether or not he comes out of his coma."

"Please, just tell me all of it—the truth."

"It's a long list already. He's been given 15 units of blood and ten of plasma, just to keep him alive. Both legs are broken, in a total of ten places. He has several fractured ribs and both arms are broken. He injured his spine and his brain, but I can't tell you how bad either of those are until we run more tests."

Theresa's eyes felt raw. Her tongue stuck to the roof of her mouth, but she remained silent.

"Now, the good news. He didn't break anything in his pelvic area and I don't believe he landed on his head. I think the brain insult is due to a secondary blow, such as when his body hit the ground. His back took the brunt of it, with his head snapping back and hitting second."

"What are his chances?" Her chin quivered in spite of her best effort to maintain control. She refused the tears that threatened to be her undoing.

"If you believe in miracles, you might want to start praying. And if I were you, I'd call in his family, anyway."

Dr. Thomas looked weary as he shrugged back into his lab coat. "I'll have someone call you periodically from the OR to give you status updates. I'll speak to you myself when it's all over."

The evening bled into night. It was 3 a.m. when the doctor pushed the swinging doors open at the end of the hall. Theresa stood.

"You've got a tough guy there, Mrs. Green. There were a couple of times I didn't know if I'd be coming out to give you good news or the worst news."

She dared to take a deep breath. "So he's doing well?"

"*Well* may be quite an optimistic adverb at this juncture. Let's just say he's still alive, in spite of everything. Every hour, every day, that passes, if he grows stronger, we can hope a little more. I just want you to be prepared if he doesn't make it."

Theresa heard her mother-in-law begin to cry and her father-in-law sniffled. She stood taller and said, "He'll make it. You just wait and see what my David can do."

The next week was a difficult one for the Greens. A funeral had to be arranged and goodbyes said to a devoted young husband and father who had died too soon. Suzanne found it hardest of all because she felt that her husband died thinking she was angry with him—and she had been.

She asked for a few minutes alone with the body. "Honey, I hope you can see me up there in Heaven. I pray that you know I love you. I'm so sorry."

* * *

David Green was stubborn in his coma, appearing to prefer the darkness to returning to a world of heartbreak. He soon developed an infection that seemed destined to take his life, in spite of the battle he'd waged up to that point. Massive amounts of IV antibiotics at last cured the infection, but David slept on.

At the end of the second month in a coma, after running pulmonary function tests, it was determined David could breathe on his own. The tube that connected him to the ventilator was removed.

Turning David's body every two hours was difficult because he was wearing what is commonly known as a *halo*, a round metal brace bolted into his skull then attached to rods that are held by a plastic vest which helps support the entire framework. Three times a day physical therapists came in and manually moved David's extremities. Theresa learned the routine and exercised her husband's arms and legs after they'd had time to heal.

This was the routine for three months. Through it all, David was cocooned in his oblivion. The hospital staff marveled at his family's perseverance. Whenever any of them mentioned it, Theresa just smiled.

"You must not be used to a patient whose family loves them as much as we love David. We're here to take care of him until he doesn't need us anymore."

Suzanne visited every day, sitting beside her brother-in-law's bed. She talked to him about the upcoming holidays, about how much he was loved, and to ask him to open his eyes.

"Come on, brother, wake up and shock the entire staff. If anyone can do this, it's you. You know me, David, I'm stubborn. I mean, I was married to your brother for a decade. If that's not stubbornness, I don't know what is. So I'm not accepting anything less than a miracle."

She took his hand and bowed her head. "Heavenly Father, I come to you today to ask you to let us have David back. Our family has lost enough. You have one of our own as your angel; please let us keep this one. Amen." She smiled, wiped her cheeks and kissed her brother-in-law's cheek. In his ear, she whispered "Okay, Davie. I did my part, now you do yours."

* * *

Theresa, Suzanne, her children, and David's parents were gathered around his bedside singing "Rudolph the Red-Nosed Reindeer" when he opened his eyes. His expression was one of alarm when he heard the group gasp, then he visibly relaxed when they all started laughing and trying to kiss his face at the same time.

Even though his voice was low, husky from lack of use, he was able to speak. "Dad, you're off key."

He couldn't turn his head but his eyes raced around the room, looking for something, for someone. Then his gaze grew somber and each person watched understanding settle in.

"He's gone, isn't he?"

Elaine Green took her son's hand and lifted it to her lips. "Yes, my love. Jimmy's gone. He's waiting for us, though."

The tears were immediate but quiet. Theresa pulled tissues from the bedside table and wiped her husband's face. He repeated the gesture his mother had just used on him; he lifted his wife's hand to kiss it. With a wife's intuition, she stepped aside when he reached for Suzanne's hand.

Whispering, he spoke earnestly. "Suze, oh Suze. Oh God, I'm so sorry. I wish it'd been me, instead. I wish …"

Her expression was stern but tempered with love. "You listen to me, David Green. Don't you ever wish that again. It wasn't your day to go to Heaven. We love Jim, we'll always miss him, but it was his time to shine. You know how he liked to sing, show off, thought he had the world's best baritone. Well, I'm sure he can now carry a tune with the best of the angels and God lets him sing lead."

She bent to hold her husband's sorrowful big brother. David's embrace was awkward due to all the equipment helping him heal, but he let her know how much he appreciated her words.

"What day is it?"

Richard Green sat on the side of the bed, next to his son. "Merry Christmas, Dave."

David's eyes again filled. "Merry Christmas, Dad. I love you. I love all of you."

With those words David fell asleep in exhaustion. Instead of a coma, this was a restful sleep that would help his body continue to heal so he could, eventually, get back to living.

It was the first day of spring when David Green returned home. He still had a long recovery ahead and his body would never be as it was before he fell from the sky, but he was now certain he would make it. David noticed the ramp covering the front porch steps and was determined to soon be free from his walker.

One step, one day, at a time.

Suspended Animation

The Rolling Stones could still put on one unbelievably exciting performance. Kendra Bostick didn't know firsthand since she couldn't afford a concert ticket, but she'd always been a huge fan. And judging by their post-concert crowd at the restaurant where she worked, they'd whipped their audience into a frenzy. She smiled at the diners' enthusiasm and laughed at their stories and attempts at singing covers for the biggest hits, but now she was glad it was over, the restaurant was closed, and she was off work. She'd had to stay later than usual to clean up because once there, it seemed no one wanted to leave. They wanted to prolong the fun evening over hamburgers and French fries. It caused her to clock out at nearly 2 a.m. instead of her usual midnight. She'd be okay after a good night's sleep and the tips were better than she'd ever made before. All in all, it had turned out to be a good day.

Because the entire area had been taken up with more cars than usual, she'd had to park nearly a half a mile away. The wind blowing off the lake cut through her thin winter coat. Maybe she could find a nice used coat at the thrift store with her extra tips. The cold lake effects from Lake Eerie made her wish she could move south for the winter, but she knew she never would because she loved Cleveland so much, no matter how cold the winters.

She wished her mother were still alive. She missed her every day. It would be wonderful to drive her little car into that garage that Mom always had open for her, lights on to guide her through the surrounding darkness. She'd get out, hit the button to close the garage door, and walk into the safe haven that smelled like Mom and cinnamon. When

Sherry Phillips had died, Kendra thought she had died with her. Not even losing her dad hurt that much.

I've got to stop thinking about that all the time. Feeling sorry for myself just makes me feel the cold that much worse. Get with the program, Kendra! Think of all that money you made tonight. Think about what kind of coat you're going shopping for tomorrow on your day off. Think about that dinner and movie date someone promised. You have a lot to be grateful for so shut down the pity party already! You've got Jerry, the best husband in the world. It's a shame that he's got that terrible cold but it does mean he'll be home when you get there, instead of at work as he usually would be. When you get home, you can take a long, hot shower, pull on your soft old "granny gown" as Jerry calls it, and cuddle up to that sweet handsome man. Yes, God's been good to you, Kendra!

The smile she'd plastered on her face faltered when she heard the first footsteps behind her. She felt her pulse quicken at the base of her throat and she stumbled a bit on the rough pavement. Stepping up her pace she dared to glance behind her, realizing the monster was ready to attack. She laughed out loud when she saw the young man and woman so wrapped up in each other she was amazed they could still walk. She watched them step into the doorway of a closed shop and could hear the murmurs and giggles of people in love. Not even the Cleveland cold could diminish the fire of their ardor.

Then a new sound, that of a boot or heavy work shoe, dragged across the icy pavement. Kendra slowed her step, listening. There, she heard it again. She stopped and whirled around, only to see a large male figure merely a few feet behind her.

Where did he come from? How did he get this close before I heard him?

Quickening her pace, Kendra's only wish was to reach the safety of her car. The man had made no menacing movement, had said nothing to frighten her, yet every fiber in her being screamed at her to run. After glancing back at the looming hulk, she did just that.

Kendra wasn't a tall person and her family had often teased that she had to take two steps to a "normal" person's one, just to keep up. Those small slender legs were doing double time at the moment. The man behind her also picked up his pace, not running, but definitely walking faster than before.

Of course, he could just be cold, he could just be anxious to get to his own car to escape the frigid temperature. Maybe he had to work late, too, and is walking fast to keep warm and hurry on home.

But Kendra felt that was decidedly not his purpose. She somehow knew *she* was his purpose.

Her lungs felt as if a fire had been ignited inside her, burning hotter with each step that she ran. Her lips were numb and her cheeks ached. The wind increased and moaned as if the entire world were in pain. Her entire body shook from the force of her heart pounding against her rib cage. Her body hummed with terror; a greasy sheen of sweat covered her body in spite of the sleet.

Kendra could see her car, imagined she could actually smell the pine tree-shaped car deodorizer hanging from the review mirror, and feel the way her foot would slip across the plastic mat beneath her accelerator when he grabbed her. Her heart stuttered within her chest and the only reason she still breathed was her autonomic nervous system.

He spun her small body around to face him and she focused on his face, trying to see if she knew him, wanting to understand who he was and why he was going to hurt her.

She didn't know him, couldn't know him because he was covered with thick, dark clothing and his face was mottled black with shadows. But she could smell him—the sweat of anger, the stink of rage, the halitosis of hatred.

Fear slammed into her, knocking hope to its knees. She felt light as air, inconsequential, when he picked her up, held her above his head for several heartbeats. Then she acknowledged all ninety-five pounds as he slammed her into the unforgiving pavement.

She lay there in the broken scaffolding of her body as he pummeled her limp body with his fists, at last straightening up to kick her, repeatedly, with those same work boots she'd heard scraping the roadway as he stalked her.

He turned to walk away but stopped when he heard an asthmatic breath escape her bruised lungs. He sighed as if having to perform a distasteful task, bent over and picked her up once again. Through the swollen eyelids which Kendra managed to open to slits, the angry clouds parted just long enough to reveal a cold moon shivering on an icy black lake just as he threw in her shattered-into-compliancy body.

Hope is hard to relinquish and she clung to hers as she lay statue-still on the top of the thin sheet of support. She had time to take one last gasp of air when she heard the splintering of the ice on the water, then inch by agonizing inch, her tiny body slid into the hungry mouth of liquid darkness.

Despite the buoyancy of the water, Kendra was unable to push herself up to the surface of the water, even if she'd been able to find the hole in the ice she'd created when she sank. Both of her arms and legs were broken, bones actually protruding through the skin in several places. With no fight left in her, it was if there was an entity in the water with her, grabbing her legs, dragging her back down to the depths from which it had come.

Several things above ground were happening quickly, frantically. The young lovers who had huddled in the open doorway of the store had seen and heard everything. Though they had both ran to Kendra's aid, they were too late to get her away from the mad man. The young man, Neil Drucker, showed bravery that most of us will never have, running directly toward the homicidal maniac. Neil's fiancée, Susan, ran behind him, cell phone open as she called for help.

Hearing their footfalls coming toward him, Lonnie Cardwell ran in the opposite direction. It seemed now that he'd accomplished what he wanted, he had no reason to linger. He veered toward Susan, perhaps to frighten her into running away, and the gray woolen scarf wrapped around his face fell down, revealing a jagged scar that ran the length of his face, from eyebrow to chin. He jerked the scarf back into place and he continued to run toward an older model VW.

Neil paced back and forth on the water's edge, yelling for the young woman he'd witnessed being thrown in, holding out his arms as if he could beseech her to swim toward the sound of his voice. Susan had begun to cry as she joined him staring into the black lake, hoping they would see Kendra.

"The cops will be here any second, Neil. They'll find her. She'll be okay."

"No, Susan, she won't be okay! She's in that freezing water and if she's not already dead, she soon will be." He pulled his coat off and he toed his shoes free of his feet.

"Neil! What are you doing? You can't jump in that water! You'll drown. Losing your own life won't save her!"

He didn't answer but instead leaned over and kissed Susan quickly, trying to infuse all the love he felt for her in that one brief moment. He walked to the water lapping at the edge of the frozen grass, took a step forward to break the ice, then slid into water that reached his knees. In a matter of seconds his teeth were chattering so hard it felt as if they would shatter. He knew he had, at the most, only minutes left to find Kendra. Soon not only would she be dead, but he would be, too. He took another step and went under.

Kendra didn't feel Neil creating currents in the water as he moved his arms around, searching for her. She didn't feel her own body swaying in those same inky currents because, for all intents and purposes, she was dead. She never heard Neil's cry of triumph when he found her limp, lifeless body. She had been completely submerged in arctic water for nearly ten minutes.

The night was illuminated by the flashing strobe lights of emergency vehicles. Policemen and paramedics ran forward to pull Neil and Kendra from what should have been their watery graves. They wrapped thermal blankets around the young man then rushed him to the warmth of the waiting ambulance.

Just before she climbed into the back of the ambulance with Neil, Susan handed a purse with a broken strap to the ambulance attendant. "This was lying on the ground, where he first grabbed her."

Kendra was covered with a aluminum-coated blanket then placed onto a separate gurney and rapidly taken to yet another ambulance. The doors slammed behind them so that the EMTs could work on the young woman who had no discernable pulse. All of her wet, frozen clothing was removed and EKG leads were placed on her bare chest while one of the first responders tried, in vain, to insert a needle for an IV. He yelled to the driver in the front, "Hyperthermia's too bad to get a line started. Let's go! We have to get this girl to the hospital if we have any chance of saving her." Under his breath he said, "Even though it's already too late. I'm sorry, honey, that we couldn't get here faster."

The two men worked like the well-conditioned medical machines that they were. One of them inserted an endotrachial tube then affixed it to an ambu bag to ventilate Kendra's lungs. He paused in his ministrations long enough for his co-worker to use paddles to shock her heart out of its tenacious state of death. The monitor still displayed a flat line. For the rest of the frantic drive over ice-bumpy roads, the paramedics alternated between CPR and the shock paddles.

Kendra still had no pulse when she arrived in ER. Doctors and nurses swarmed Kendra like she was the queen bee in the world's largest hive. Each staff member had a specific job and did it well. Because the frigid water had caused vasoconstriction, the first thing done was to insert a catheter into a large vein in her neck, to be used to inject medication or fluids, and to obtain blood and cardiovascular measurements.

In the midst of all this, the doctors and nurses working to resuscitate Kendra heard a strident voice, demanding to be heard.

"I'm looking for my wife. Kendra. That's her name. Kendra Bostick. Somebody called me; told me she was here. Please, someone help me!"

Hospital personnel have been trained to be compassionate but keep distance between themselves and people who may be on the verge of losing control. Jerry seemed to be skittering close to the edge. The nurse behind the desk leaned over to place her hand across his; her expression illustrated she understood his terror.

"Jerry? My name is Denise. I'm the one who called you. Let's go to the family waiting room and we'll talk there, okay?"

She put her arm around the man's trembling shoulders and guided him down the hall. She waited until he sat down before she began talking. "Remember, I'm a nurse so there's only so much I can tell you. Doctor Decker will be here soon and he can give you the details."

"What happened? All you said on the phone was that Kendra was hurt, in critical condition, and to get here right away. I nearly clipped a few telephone poles trying to hurry. I couldn't speed; the roads are too icy. What if she'd died while I was driving so slow?" His voice began to rise in register, his eyes growing even larger. Denise sat down beside him and took his hand.

"Kendra was walking to her car when she was attacked."

"Attacked? What do you mean-attacked? Who did it? Did he hurt her? Well of course he hurt her or she wouldn't be so critical, right? Did he … oh my God, did he …?"

"No! He didn't rape her."

"How can you be so sure? Have they checked her … you know …"

"There were witnesses."

"Witnesses? If there were witnesses, didn't they even try to help her? Did they just stand there and let someone hurt Kendra?"

"Jerry, take a deep breath and let me speak." Denise sat still as he forced himself to sit up straighter, take a slow, jagged breath. They both turned when the door opened.

Dr. Decker was a tall, slender man who wore the gray streaks at his temples with distinction. If you stopped your perusal at his chest you were quite impressed. Allowing your gaze to move downward, you might have been put off by the smears of vivid red blood on his lab coat.

Jerry immediately stood, as it seems most family members do when they're scared of what they're going to hear. Dr. Decker motioned for him to be reseated and smiled at the nurse. Denise discreetly slipped from the room.

"Okay, tell me the truth, Doc. I don't even know what happened to get her here. All I know is she was attacked ..."

Decker took the seat that Denise had vacated and looked into Jerry's face. He took a deep breath, releasing it slowly.

"Yes, Kendra was attacked. The assault was one of the most vicious I've ever dealt with. Both arms and legs are broken in several places. In five places there is bone protruding through the skin. She has a hairline skull fracture, all of her ribs were kicked in, and her jaw is so broken she'll be wired shut for quite some time, if she survives."

Jerry jumped up as if his seat had caught fire. "If she survives? You think she won't make it?"

Dr. Decker took Jerry's wrist to guide him back to his seat. "While the injuries she has are egregious, in themselves capable of causing catastrophic consequences, they are not her only problem."

Tears began to slide unchecked down Jerry's cheeks. He stared at Decker, silently urging him to continue. The doctor pulled in a longer, deeper breath than before.

"Kendra also drowned."

The husband fell back against the cushions of the sofa, unable to voice another question. His brows met across his nose and his eyes squinted in confusion.

"From what I've been told, she was totally submerged underwater for nearly ten minutes. By all accounts, Jerry, she should be dead; should've been DOA, but she is still alive. You owe the paramedics and the man who dove in to save her a huge debt of gratitude. If Kendra lives, especially if she has minimal brain damage, it is solely due to their heroic efforts. I merely took over, with expensive machines, what they'd already begun out there in the snow and ice."

"I don't understand, Doc. If she drowned, how can she still be alive?" He stopped, stared at the floor then looked back to the doctor. "Oh, God—she drowned!"

"As the temperature falls, the body shunts blood away from the skin and exposure to the elements. Blood flow is increased to the vital organs of the body including the heart, lungs, kidneys, and brain. The heart and brain are most sensitive to cold, and the electrical activity in these organs slows in response to cold. If the body temperature continues to decrease, organs begin to fail, and eventually death will occur. There have been documented cases where someone has survived being underwater even longer than Kendra. Right now we'll continue what we're doing and hope for the best."

Jerry dropped his face into his hands.

"And Jerry? If you're a believer, you might want to pray."

"I haven't stopped since I got the call..."

"Right now, it's in His hands. We'll do everything we can to save her, but man can only do so much." He patted the distraught man on the shoulder. "Jerry, you might want to call in her family."

Dr. Decker shut his eyes tight as he closed the door on the man's harsh sobs.

* * *

The days turned into weeks and the group of loving support that occupied the family waiting room dwindled down to a solitary husband who slept on the hard plastic sofas and woke at dawn to rush home and get ready for work. After work he'd grab dinner from a drive-through window and scarf it down during the drive to his second home, Memorial Hospital.

After two months, Kendra remained in a medicated fog. Jerry wasn't sure she even knew he was there beside her, but that was okay, *he* knew.

Dr. Decker smiled when he saw the young husband holding his wife's hand.

"Jerry, I have a tiny bit of good news. We're going to move Kendra to what we call a 'step down' unit. She isn't sick enough for ICU but is still too ill for a 'regular' room. The big difference will be that you can spend more time with her. You can even have a cot across the room from your wife. What do you think of that?"

"It's the happiest I've been since the night before I was summoned to the ER."

"I don't want you to get your hopes up too high, Jerry, but it looks as if your girl here is fighting hard to make progress. I think it'll be good for her recovery to get out of this unit. Who knows, having her husband around might make her *want* to come back. I know her husband is sure anxious to have his wife home where she belongs."

"Well Doc, I guess I'll just have to pray a little harder. After all, I don't want Him to forget about her."

Decker grinned. "Jerry, I doubt if you'd ever let that happen."

* * *

The days droned on with the only change being that Jerry now got to sleep in the same room with Kendra. Some days he raced to her side after work; some days he took the long way around the city. Hope may spring eternal for some, but all of us have our doubts. Standing beside her bed, looking into Kendra's unhinged gaze of the ceiling left a bitter taste in Jerry's mouth. He prayed for one, just one, sign.

"Please, God. She's fighting but she can't break free. Please step in, take her hand, and guide her out. We've done all we can do; it's all up to You now."

Dr. Decker and his nurse were waiting for Jerry when he walked into his wife's room. Jerry's heart leaped into his throat and he felt sweat dot his forehead. He didn't take a deep breath until he saw the doctor begin to smile.

"Hey, Jerry, welcome to the party! Come see what Kendra can do!"

Jerry covered the remaining few feet of floor space quickly. He stopped and gasped when Kendra turned her eyes to look at him. In seconds, her face was suffused with light, her eyes widened, and she opened her mouth to smile as she always did when she saw her husband. She lifted her hand, not quite managing to get it off the sheet, but the movement was obvious.

Jerry leaned over and covered her faces with kisses. The musical chimes of her laughter lifted the stone that had crushed his heart since that long-ago winter night. He lifted his head to stare into her eyes, to amaze at her smile.

"Baby? Oh Kendra, you're back! I've missed you so much. Thank you, God, for bringing my girl back to me!"

* * *

Physical therapy was long, hard, painful and frustrating. There were times when Kendra lost her temper and said she quit, that she couldn't do it anymore. But those blowouts were few, tepid, and short in duration. The PT would pick up a magazine and give Kendra time to vent. Then when Kendra started laughing, they'd get back to the workout.

It took them four months to find Lonnie Cardwell. Susan, now wife of the man who pulled Kendra from the frozen lake, had given the police an excellent description of the man, his car, and license plate number. They were amazed at how calm she'd remained or she never would have been able to remember all the details. Therefore, the police had known from the first few days following the assault just who they were looking for, but actually locating him was a whole other problem. They'd found a couple of friends whose only cooperation was to tell authorities that "Poor ol' Lonnie had been flying high that night, man! He didn't mean to hurt that girl. He thought she was Sandra, his girlfriend that had ripped off all his drugs and money. He just got mixed up, man, that's all." That's all ... as if it would've been okay for Lonnie to attempt to kill another woman who might have been considered by some to be a lower caliber than Kendra Bostick.

The beginning of the end was at a red light near the same lake where Cardwell had thrown Kendra. He was driving a different car but, being high again, Lonnie lost it when a cop car pulled behind him to wait for the light to turn green. Paranoia pushed Cardwell through the red light, so he felt justified when the light bar and siren were turned on behind him. He gunned his car and outran the police for nearly a mile until he reached a curve he couldn't maneuver. He stomped the brakes, but the momentum of the heavy machine propelled both car and driver through a guardrail and out into the lake. When they pulled the car from the water, Lonnie still sat behind the steering wheel, held in place by his seat belt, his eyes blared in fear of the death he knew had caught up with him.

* * *

Leaves covered the streets as Jerry drove Kendra home at last.

"Wow! I went into the hospital in the winter and it's nearly winter again. Gee, time flies when you're having fun, right, Jerry?"

"Sweetheart, we have a whole lifetime still ahead of us. You ready for this? I'm still worried you're not up to a big family celebration."

"Hey, I was beaten and drowned, meant to die, but I beat all the odds. I have reason to celebrate! C'mon Jerry, let's go begin the rest of our lives!"

Mirror Images

In the corner of his eye, he saw her sneaking up behind him. He pretended as if he didn't. She would quickly find the tables turned when she was the one frightened out of her mind.

That's right; just a little closer. Come on. Atta girl!

When she was within inches, he twirled around and began tickling her ribcage. She started squirming and laughing so hard she dropped the thing she held behind her back.

Michael let her go and bent down to pick up the purple and white stick. Lorna's laughing subsided. He stood up, looked at her with his head bent to the side and a puzzled look on his face.

"I know that look, Michael Miller. Why so confused? You've seen a pregnancy test before."

"Yes I have, I'm just not sure I'm reading this one right."

"Well, honey, it only has one word on it so that it's so simple even a man can read it!" Her laughter bubbled out of proportion to the teasing she was administering to her husband of ten years.

"It says ... Lorna, it says ..."

She threw her arms around him and kissed him hard. "Yes, Michael, it says we're going to have a baby!"

They danced around the bedroom for a few seconds until Michael stopped so abruptly he nearly fell, holding onto Lorna as if to steady her before she toppled over with him in a heap on the floor. He stood stock-still, staring into her face, his own eyes large and round in a face quickly losing all color.

"We can't be doing that, Lorna! We can't be dancing around like we have springs on our feet. It might do something to the baby."

"What, like jar it loose? Honey, I'm a better shock absorber than that!"

"Well, the other times ..."

"Those didn't happen because we danced for joy, Michael, they happened because ..."

He held her to his chest and kissed the top of her head. "Yes honey, I know."

Lorna leaned back in his arms and smiled through her tears. "This little girl is tough; I can just tell. You'll be screening boyfriends before you know it."

"Oh really? And just how do you know it's a girl? I think that before I know it, I'll be the one in the bleachers screaming, 'That's my boy!'"

"And then he'll look at the camera and say, 'Hi Mom!'"

Michael picked Lorna up and twirled her around as he laughed. "We'll see about that, 'Mom!'"

She disentangled herself to pick up the phone to make an appointment with her doctor.

"You have an opening tomorrow at 3:00?" She looked to see Michael nodding his head enthusiastically. "Okay, we'll be there!"

* * *

Lorna smoothed the paper gown down to her knees as she sat on the side of the examination table. She was always happy when she could release her feet from the stirrups.

"Lorna, I estimate you're nearly eight weeks. I wish you'd come in sooner."

"After the other times, I felt, well, I ..."

Michael took her hand in his. "Doc, I think she was afraid she'd jinx herself. She'd only missed one period and she wanted to be more confident of herself." He smiled as Lorna nodded and squeezed his hand in gratitude.

"I can understand that, Lorna. Get this prescription filled for prenatal vitamins and start them immediately. I'll call you tomorrow afternoon with the results of your blood work, but I think everything looks fine. Don't stop living, but do everything in moderation. I want the baby to thrive but I want a healthy mother, too. Michael, take care of that for me, will you?"

The answering grin could light up the darkest street in any town. "You can count on me, Doc!"

Walking down the street after leaving the doctor's office, Michael felt a tug on his hand that had been holding Lorna's smaller one.

"What is it, honey? Is something wrong?"

"No, nothing's wrong, Michael, but you look like the cat that ate the canary with that big ol' goofy smile plastered all over your face."

"Hey, I have every reason in the world to be wearing this goofy smile. And all the expectant fathers are wearing them now. It's the latest fashion rage, or hadn't you noticed?"

"Is that so? Well, far be it from me to advise such a fashion icon as yourself, Michael Miller. I'll just walk beside you and pretend I don't notice everyone staring at you."

"They're only staring because I'm walking with the most beautiful pregnant woman in the world."

"Wow, I didn't realize that. Okay, then; carry on!"

As chance would have it, they were standing in front of a baby boutique. Michael was salivating over a small soft football in the window display. He grinned as he started into the store when he once again felt the tug on his arm.

"No honey, please, not yet. I feel as if it's tempting fate. Let's wait until I'm a little further along before we buy anything for our *daughter*; who, by the way, may or may not, appreciate a football!"

The next few weeks were blessedly uneventful with Lorna taking her vitamins as promised and Michael hovering over her to the point of occasional irritation, also as promised.

The next visit to the doctor's office had them walking on Cloud Nine.

"Well, here's a nice surprise for you both. How do you feel about having twins?"

Lorna began to cry and Michael laughed out loud. "How do we feel? Thank you, God, that's how we feel!" He leaned down and kissed his wife soundly. "I guess we better go buy two footballs now, honey."

His wife chuckled and told the doctor, "Michael's just certain that we're having a son. Well, we might have two girls, Mr. Miller! How do you like that?"

Dr. Tillman clapped Michael on the back. "Well, sir, you should've bet on that one!"

The couple froze, then began to weep as they smiled. Michael was the first to find his voice.

"Oh Lorna—boys! We're going to have two sons!"

It was another two months before Michael and Lorna's earth tilted on its axis. It began with a routine ultrasound that proved anything but routine was going to be the agenda for the rest of the pregnancy.

"Lorna, Michael, I want to talk to you about what the ultrasound images are showing. I hate to have to tell you this."

Lorna took Michael's shaking hand into both of her cold ones. They glanced at each other quickly then turned their full attention back to the physician, their breath held in suspended fear.

Dr. Tillman pulled in a deep breath. "The babies have what we call TTTS, or Twin to Twin Transfusion Syndrome. It's a condition in which the twins are connected by blood vessels. I'll be honest with you; it's not good."

Lorna touched the physician's hand as if contact would lend a lie to his words. When his expression didn't change, her eyes filled with tears. "What does this mean? Did I do something wrong, something to hurt my babies?"

The doctor pulled a stool closer to the terrified mother and took her hand from Michael.

"The early pregnancy events responsible for TTTS are in place before the mother knows she is pregnant, which means there is no primary prevention for TTTS. It is not caused by hereditary, genetics or by anything you did or did not do, nor is it caused by anything the babies are doing because they are innocent bystanders to events in their placenta."

Michael's voice shook as he asked, "Can you tell us what it means, in a way that we can understand?"

Dr. Tillman used his free hand to cover the father's hand on his rapidly bouncing knee. "TTTS is a disease that strikes about 10% of all identical twin pregnancies. This serious condition occurs when twins share a single placenta, which contains blood vessels connecting the twins' blood streams. In a sense, they are like conjoined twins, but are connected in the placenta instead of their bodies. One baby, the recipient, may get too much blood, while the other, the donor, is losing blood through the abnormal connections."

Lorna whispered, "What does that do to the babies?"

The OB/GYN sighed. "I'm going to give it to you straight. The recipient may die in heart failure from a cardiovascular system overload, and subsequent over-production of quarts of amniotic fluid. The donor may die from the loss of blood, and tends to have very little amniotic fluid. While the twins begin development totally normal, the placenta abnormalities cause their subsequent death or cause serious birth defects. The loss rate may be as high as 80 to 100 percent for twins who develop TTTS at mid-pregnancy, or the second trimester, which is where you are, Lorna. The babies may die in the uterus or at birth from prematurity. More than half of those who survive suffer from many serious birth defects including cerebral palsy. In other words, one twin literally drains the life out of the other. Left untreated, there is an 80 to 90 percent that both babies will die."

"If left untreated ... what's the treatment?" Her voice wavered on the last syllables.

"I suggest that you consider unfortunately limited options. First of all, you can terminate one pregnancy, or both. Or do nothing and let the pregnancy naturally evolve into a miscarriage."

Lorna was shaking her head fast enough to cause her hair to hang in her eyelashes even before the sentence was completed. Michael just held her hand as she left no doubt that this was not an option.

"Then I think we should reduce the excess amniotic fluid that has developed around the recipient baby, done via amniocenteses. There's a 50 percent chance this procedure might balance the amount of amniotic fluid surrounding each baby and hopefully spur the placenta into regularity once again."

"What if that doesn't correct it?" Lorna had clearly decided to fight with everything in a mother's arsenal.

"The next option would be an in-utero surgery called fetoscopic laser occlusion of the connecting vessels. But I have to warn you, that if you are going to attempt to carry these babies, we should remove the excess fluid today, immediately. Because of the situation's urgency, time is a tight commodity for us right now."

Michael's face portrayed all the anxiety and love he possessed. "Honey? What do you think?"

Lorna placed her hand on her husband's face and without looking away from him, said, "Dr. Tillman, I'm ready when you are."

After removing over one and half liters of fluid, Dr. Tillman told Lorna to go home and stay in bed for the next four days.

"I'll call you to check your progress while I make a few calls to a specialist I've read about. I don't feel comfortable in proceeding past amniocentesis fluid reduction in this case. I'll keep you informed of what I find out. Of course, if you have any type of problem, no matter how trivial you may think it to be, go to the hospital emergency room as fast as you can."

* * *

Being an active person, lying in bed hours on end was difficult for Lorna but she was determined to give her babies every chance she could.

The next evening the phone rang and Michael answered it before coming into the bedroom where she lay, the cordless phone to his ear.

"Yes, Dr. Lyons, I'm here with her now. I'm going to put you on speaker so we can both hear what you have to say."

"Lorna, hello, my name is David Lyons and I'm calling you at the request of Dr. Tillman. I understand you and your babies are in trouble."

Lorna's eyes grew moist at the word *trouble*.

"Yes Dr. Lyons, were certainly are. Can you help us?"

"Michael, grab a pen and paper to take notes. I've got a few ideas and quite a bit of information to give you. Lorna, the first order of business is for you to remain where you are—in bed. I want you to begin drinking a dietary supplement, something like Ensure or Boost. Your blood work shows you're becoming anemic and you want to be strong enough to fight for those boys growing inside you."

Michael jerked so hard on a nightstand drawer, looking for pen and paper, the drawer pulled free and hit the floor with a loud thud. He grinned sheepishly at Lorna who smiled and slightly shook her head.

The voice on the other end of the speaker sounded hollow. "Michael? You didn't pass out on me, did you?"

Lorna laughed. "No, he's just trying to destroy the furniture. His kingdom for a pencil! Okay, Dr. Lyons, he now has something to write on and something to write with. We're ready."

"Until you reach a certain gestational age, you may have to have amniotic fluid reduction again. If fluid reduction doesn't fix the problem, then we'll operate, using a small 3.5 millimeter scope to identify the connecting vessels, then use the laser to coagulate them. The twins would then become separate and the passage of blood from one to the other stops. This surgery is performed in 'pre-viable' pregnancies, less than 25 weeks, where delivery of the TTTS twins is not an option. So, for now, drink the supplements, stay in bed, and continue the amniocenteses, if necessary. Remember that your twins would only be candidates for the laser surgery if they meet certain criteria, which include severe size differences between them or evidence of impending heart failure. I'll be in touch with you and Dr. Tillman and hope that we never have to actually meet. That would mean that the simple measures would correct the condition and make surgery unnecessary."

A week later Lorna had to have another amnioreduction, removing nearly one liter of fluid. That's when it was determined that the twins' condition was worsening. The recipient's heart muscle was thickening and the outlook was bleaker than they imagined. It was then that Lorna and Michael felt it was time to call in Dr. Lyons; Dr. Tillman fully agreed.

Dr. Lyons arrived the next morning as Lorna was being prepped for surgery. He came into her room and shook Michael's hand.

"Well, kids, I'd hoped it wouldn't come to this. You seem like nice people but I really wish I didn't have to meet you, at least, not under these circumstances." He smiled and put his hand on Lorna's shoulder. "How are you feeling, Mama? Ready for surgery?"

Her voice trembled, "As ready as I can be. All I want to do is give my boys a chance to live."

"That's exactly how I feel, too, Mrs. Miller. Now here comes the part that some people don't agree with but I feel it's as necessary as the anesthesia they'll be using in the operating room."

Michael's eyes were opened wide and his face pale. Lorna forced a confidant smile but neither one asked what he meant.

"Lorna, I don't know what your religious leanings are and it truly isn't important that I do know, but mine is that I pray before every procedure I perform. I believe I only have the knowledge and skill that God gave me and I always ask Him to assist me in the operating room. I've never done surgery without Him and I don't intend to today."

Michael cried openly and Lorna covered Dr. Lyons' hand with her own. "That's what we were doing when you walked into the room. We wouldn't even consider going into surgery without Him, either."

There were some ups and downs, some good days and some not so good, following that surgery. It was all worth it, when, fifteen weeks later the Miller boys were welcomed into the world of intensive care, terrified parents, harried nurses, and two doctors who had never been confident of their survival.

They are now strong, healthy, loud boys who like nothing more than giggling every time their father misses a football pass.

For more information, or to donate, visit the Twin to Twin Syndrome Foundation web address at:

http://www.tttsfoundation.org

Superhero

"Logan, come on! Tom? Hey, guys, push the pause button and let's eat. Time for dinner."

From the other room she heard an abrupt silence as the movie was paused, followed by a low groaning.

"Aw, Daddy, it was getting to the good part, too!"

"The good part that you've seen a million times already? You already know what's going to happen, Logan."

"Yeah, I know but ..."

"After we help Mommy clean up the dinner dishes we can go back to see the good part, okay?"

Logan's small lips were turned downward and he shuffled his feet, his blue cape hanging in long folds at his back.

"Wow, I never saw a super hero act like that." Logan didn't look up at his mother. "C'mon, Super Britches, perk up. I made chicken nuggets—your favorite."

Logan raised his head and she saw a face identical to her husband's wreathed in a big smile.

"Aw, Mom, my name ain't Super Britches."

"Oh no? What is your name again?"

His four year old laughter made her heart swell. "Aw, you know my name. I'm Super Duper Duper Boy!" He looked at his father and shook his head in consternation. "Daddy, Mommy's acting like she don't know my name. Ain't that silly?"

Tom grinned at Hailey as he gave her a brief hug. He answered his son while looking into her shining blue eyes. "Why, yes, I believe you're right, Logan. Mommy is a silly girl."

Hailey playfully punched his bicep. "Silly Mommy is going to make Daddy sorry for that remark. Just for that, oh, Father of Super Duper Duper Boy, you have to finish cutting that broken limb on that tree right after supper."

Tom's face fell in mock disappointment. "But Mooom, I wanted to finish watching the movie with my side-kick, Super Kid."

Logan looked up at the ceiling and shook his head slowly. "Daaaad, that ain't my name! My name is ..."

Tom smacked his forehead. "Oh, yeah, your name is Super Duper Boy. I'm sorry. I'm getting old and I forget things like that."

"Noooo, it's Super Duper *Duper* Boy! You left out a Duper, Dad!"

Hailey lifted Logan and said, "Okay, Mr. SDDB, kindly hold that cape out so you won't sit on it when I put you down. I don't know how good a seamstress I am so those stitches might just pop right out if you tug on the cape."

Logan did as he was told and Tom watched with a happy smile. "That was pretty nice of Mommy to make you that really cool super hero outfit, wasn't it, Lo?"

The little boy smiled up at his mother and nodded enthusiastically. "It sure was. It was super duper duper nice of her."

Hailey shook her own head and chuckled. "Okay, enough already! Logan, will you please say the blessing, honey?"

"Rub-a-dub-dub, thanks for the grub! Amen!"

Hailey's eyes grew larger with each syllable and Tom kept his eyes closed and head bowed. She saw the twinges playing at the corners of his lips.

"Logan! Where did you hear that?"

Logan quickly turned a startled look at his father. Tom opened his eyes and said, "Yes, Logan, where did you hear such a thing?"

"But Daddy, you said ..."

"I said you should say grace the right way. Now, try it again, son."

Tears began to fill Logan's eyes and Tom pushed his chair back to reach his son. "Oh, buddy, it's okay. Mommy's not really mad. Are you, Mommy? She knows Daddy was just playing a little joke on her, to make her laugh."

Logan sniffled and looked up at his mother from beneath eyelashes glistening with teardrops. "Is that right, Mommy? You know Daddy was just playing and told me to say that and you're not mad at me?"

Hailey went to the other side of Logan's chair and wrapped her arms around the little boy. "Oh, sweetie, no, I'm not mad. I was just so surprised that Daddy taught you that and you remembered every single word without any help. That shows that Daddy worked with you for quite awhile to get it just right."

"Yes, he did, Mommy. We worked hard to get it right. Did you like it, Mommy? Do you think it's funny?"

"Oh, Logan, that's the funniest thing I've heard since my wedding day. Now, how about you say the real grace for Mommy, okay?"

The adults went back to their seats and when Logan saw they were not angry and their heads were bowed once again, he gave it another try.

"Thank you for the food we eat. Thank you for the world so sweet. Thank you for the birds that sing. Thank you God for everything. Amen."

When his parents both smiled at him, all was good in Logan's world.

"I'm awful hungry. What's that stuff, Mommy? That's not ..." he gasped dramatically, "kryptonite, is it?"

Tom laughed until the milk he'd just taken a sip of blew through pursed lips. "No. Logan, but it probably tastes just as bad."

Hailey rolled her eyes. "Oh, Lord, that boy's going to be on stage. He's just too dramatic for words. Logan, that's broccoli and it tastes very good. I want you to try a bite."

Logan squinted his eyes closed, leaned forward, and opened his mouth, a little. Hailey grinned at his expression and put a small piece of the green vegetable in his mouth.

Logan closed his lips, chewed slowly at first, then began to chew faster as he fought a gag reflex. Tom laughed out loud and picked up a napkin, holding it beneath his son's mouth.

"Okay, buddy, spit it in here. At least you tried, right Mom?"

Hailey's smile was rueful as she nodded. "Yes, honey, you tried. I guess broccoli's just not your favorite food."

Logan spit the chewed green mess into the paper napkin, then grabbed another one to wipe his tongue vigorously.

"Oh, that tastes bad, Mommy. I'd rather eat kryptonite!"

The rest of the meal was uneventful. Logan prattled on about his favorite subject, super heroes. Whenever he took a breath, his parents discussed the large limb to be removed from the old beech tree next to the driveway. It had been a bone of contention between them for weeks and they argued about Tom not wanting to simply remove the limb.

"I still think we should call someone out to cut that thing down."

"No, Tom, I don't want to do that. I don't want to lose the whole tree. It's just that one limb. I don't see the big deal with just climbing up there and cutting it off. Besides, we can't afford to get someone else to do it."

"I suppose the height is what bothers me. I mean, that tree has to be nearly 60 feet tall and that broken branch is near the top. I'm pretty sure I can reach it. At least, I think I can."

She ran her hand across her face. "Honey, will you at least try to do it, yourself?"

"Yeah, yeah, yeah. I've already got the ladder out there. I told you I'd do it after dinner."

"Thanks, honey. I just don't want it to fall on one of our cars or, worse yet, I don't want it to fall on Logan at some point."

Logan made a half-hearted swipe with the dishcloth across the dining table, then turned to his mom with a big smile plastered on his face. "All done! Can I go watch the movie now?"

Hailey reached over to playfully ruffle his soft brown curls. "Tell you what, champ, why don't you go out and play for a bit? You watch way too much TV. Daddy's going to help Mommy clean up the kitchen and then we'll both come outside with you. Then later, after you have your bath and get on your pajamas, we'll all sit down and finish the movie. How does that sound to you?"

Logan jumped down from the table and saluted his mother. "That sounds just peachy, Super Duper Duper Mommy!" He ran out of the room, nearly colliding with the unsuspecting cat walking toward her own dinner.

The couple laughed. "Well, I wonder where in the world he heard something like that. And what's with the salute?"

"Oh, who knows? I'm sure he saw it on a commercial or a movie. You're right, Hailey, he watches too much television. I'm going to start making a more concentrated effort to get him outside and play in the sunshine. It's healthier for his mind and body."

They worked together at the sink. Tom rinsed the dishes and Hailey loaded the dishwasher. They teased each other the way that married couples sometimes do and the house was filled with their shared love.

It took about ten minutes to finish, and it was then that Hailey realized she hadn't seen Logan in the backyard for a few minutes.

"Where'd Logan go? Tom, have you seen him?"

"Not in awhile, but he hasn't gone anywhere. The yard's fenced and the gate's locked. He can't get out of the yard. I'm going to go out there and climb that ladder that's standing next to the tree and see if I ..."

Hailey ran for the door, calling out as she did.

"Logan? Logan, where are you?" She hit the storm door with enough force to slam it against the side of the house.

As if sounding from a long distance, they both heard, "Mommy! I'm right here!"

She stopped just long enough to stare into her husband's eyes. "Oh, God, no!" They both began to run to the side of the house. Instinctively they both looked toward the beech tree.

"Hey, Daddy, look at me! I'm way up high! Can you see me, Mommy? I'm all the way up in the clouds!"

There, near the top of the tree, stood a small boy in a super hero costume. The branch on which he stood balancing was bending even under his light weight; the wind caused it to sway due to its small diameter.

Hailey stifled a scream as she reached her arms toward her son and saw him fall. The cape unfurled in the wake of his furious descent. His freefall seemed at once in slow motion, and then it hurled fast forward. Though she was transfixed, Tom's frightened yell uprooted her and they both ran toward their son.

Logan's small body snapped limbs as he fell. His cries of horror stopped after he broke the third branch with his weight. Hailey's heart felt as if it stopped and a fist was crammed into her abdomen when she saw her son's forehead slam against the broken branch that had caused all the trouble. When she heard, as well as saw, his head snap back on his neck, it felt as if someone had shoved a fist down her throat. Next to her, she heard Tom whisper, "Oh please, God, no."

Small boys hitting the ground from fifty feet up make no more than a muffled thudding sound when they hit the ground. The broken branches rained down upon Logan's still form and pelted the heads of his parents who knelt beside him.

"Tom, call for help! And tell them to hurry!" Her voice rose to near a scream on the last word.

The sirens brought neighbors from their homes to see what had happened. They stood in a large circle around the young family surrounded by broken limbs and crumpled leaves.

The paramedics gently, so gently, slid a brace around Logan's slender neck, then put a flat backboard against the child's back and turned him over with agonizing slowness. Hailey felt like she would pummel them if they didn't move faster, faster, faster. Then they scarcely took time to check his vitals before running with their small charge.

Tom and Hailey had tried to climb in the back with their son, but the paramedic working on Logan shook his head. "Please, Mr. and Mrs. Miller, I know you want to go with him but since I have to work fast and it's so cramped in here, would you please just meet us at Mercy West?" Without waiting for a response he yelled through the small window separating him from the driver. "Let's go, Brian. We need to get this little boy to the hospital STAT!"

* * *

A resident was waiting for Tom and Hailey when they arrived at the hospital. He kindly steered them to a private room.

"Mr. and Mrs. Miller, my name is Dr. Stokes and my only function at this moment is to speak to you about your son. He's being examined by Dr. Felicia Rhodes, the best trauma surgeon in the city."

"May we see him? How is he? Is he awake? Will he ..."

"Mrs. Miller, while I can't say that I understand how you feel, I can appreciate your concern. As I have yet to see Logan, and the attending has had little time to do much more than a cursory exam, I have precious little to tell you. Here's what I know at this moment: Logan is still unconscious. He had spontaneous respiration when he arrived, but after that he had to be intubated and placed on a ventilator."

Tom dropped into a chair and put his head in his hands. Hailey remained standing, though she was trembling so hard it would seem she would collapse at any second.

"I know this all sounds scary because it *is* scary. I'm afraid that I now have to join Dr. Rhodes. As soon as we have any news, one of us will come out to speak to you. I know it's easier said than done, but please be patient with us. We'll work as fast as we can, but we don't want to miss something important to Logan's care."

With that he was gone and Hailey finally allowed herself to fall into the seat next to Tom. There they sat, holding hands, crying, praying, and watched the hands crawl around the face of the clock on the wall.

Dr. Rhodes was an impressive figure. She was tall and slim with a commanding countenance that seemed to gentle when she offered a smile. It was just a small smile but the Millers would cling to anything that appeared to be a positive sign. She leaned toward them, as if to make sure she had their full attention, something she'd had the moment she opened the door.

Hailey took the doctor's hand and looked into her eyes. "Is Logan alive?"

"Yes, he's alive. He even woke up in the exam room, briefly. As you were told, he's on a machine that breathes for him since he can't do it on his own."

Tom's shoulders drooped.

"I'll warn you ahead of time that this is critical. I'm not going to sugarcoat it because I want you to completely understand what I'm saying. I would think that seeing your son hit so many branches as he fell caused your heart to tighten. But the very thing that should've killed him may be the very thing that kept him alive. From what I understand, he must have been fifty feet or more off the ground."

Tom nodded in agreement but didn't utter a sound.

"If there had been nothing to slow down his momentum, something like those branches, if he'd fallen directly from that height, I doubt we'd even be having a conversation. In all likelihood, he would have been a DOA and you would have signed forms before someone took him to the morgue."

Hailey gasped as tears dripped onto her lap.

"I hit you with that scenario so you can see how it *could* have gone. Maybe by realizing he could have died, you'll understand how lucky your child is and you can hang onto that because his condition is still grave. In fact, he's a very, very sick little boy."

The doctor reached up to pull the surgical cap from her head, then massaged the muscles of her right shoulder.

"Logan had an atlanto-occipital dislocation, or an internal decapitation."

The parents were frozen, pinned to their chairs by terror.

"An orthopedic decapitation is an extremely rare condition where the skull actually separates from the spinal column. The reason I say Logan is lucky is that this is nearly always fatal, since it involves nerve damage or severance of the spinal cord. It had to be a perfect storm of injuries for Logan to survive such a horrific injury."

Tom put his arm around his wife and cleared his throat. "Is Logan going to be okay? Will he have, I mean, will he be ..."

"Mr. Miller, I can't give you an honest answer about whether or not Logan will ever again be the same little boy who climbed into that tree today. I can't even promise you that he will live. Right now, he's in intensive care with a Halo brace around his skull just to hold his head immobile. We're trying to keep him stable and see how much swelling there will be. You can visit him for a few minutes, but know that he's non-responsive now because we have sedated him heavily. The plan is to take him into surgery, hopefully tomorrow, to affix however many plates and screws it takes to stabilize his head. But I'm not making a move until I see how he progresses through the night. Folks, try to prepare yourselves. If your son survives, he's in for the fight of his life. He will have months of rehab ahead of him with no guarantee that he'll ever walk, talk or live what we consider a 'normal' life again. I truly wish I had better news for you. Do you have any questions?"

The heartbroken mother stared at the floor as she answered. "I don't think that we'd even know what questions to ask. Just please promise me you'll do all that you can and I promise you that we'll do whatever Logan needs."

The little caped crusader went into surgery the next afternoon to reattach his skull to his spinal cord. Later, when Dr. Rhodes showed the Millers the post-op x-rays; they were amazed at how many screws their child had inside his small body to hold him together.

* * *

The first six months showed a remarkable amount of improvement, with few setbacks. Youth was on Logan's side, helping him to physically heal quicker. With each week that passed, he gained more strength and his rehabilitation became more intense. There were times Logan became frustrated when he tried to speak—or mad when the washers were slid tighter on the halo screws.

The staff helped Logan celebrate his fifth birthday, decorating his room with balloons, cards, and dozens of gifts. His mother gave him the present which created his largest smile. He ran his hands over the smooth lines of the red cape attached to the blue pullover shirt.

Dr. Rhodes walked in with her own gift just as Logan was admiring his new hero clothes.

"Look, Dr. R ... R ... Rho! Mommy made me a new costume."

"Wow, will you look at that? I think that's probably just the coolest cape I've ever seen. But Logan, will you promise me to never climb anything else like a tree again? You're going to be good as new in a few more months, but I want you to always be careful, and take it easy."

Logan lifted an arm and saluted her. "Bet on it, Doc! Super Duper Duper Boy is grounded!"

Pin-up Model

The sun was shining brightly in Karensa Patton's world. Officially, a high school senior in the fall, she was going to enjoy this summer, her last summer as a carefree "kid". Next summer, she'd be busy working to help pay for the books she'd need to become a student at Rice University. It would be a long drive from her home in northeastern Oklahoma to Houston and she would miss her family, but in her secret heart of hearts, she was thrilled at the prospect of being away from home and becoming independent.

She and her mother had set up this tour of the Houston campus. Karensa's excitement grew with each step as they walked. Her mother noticed the young men turning to take a second look at her tall, willowy daughter. Even though it tugged at her, she understood why they would notice the beautiful face, waist-length blond hair and large green eyes. She only hoped that Karensa would fixate more on subjects other than the anatomy of the male species.

"What are you laughing about, Mom?"

"I was just hoping you remember to study something other than biology when you get here."

"Oh, Mom, that's crazy! I'm going to Rice to shape my future—make something of my life. I worked hard all of my life to get that scholarship. I'm sure not going to mess that up when I finally get here. But that's not to say I won't date a boy, or two, or three ..." She laughed out loud at her mother's pretended look of shock.

"I'm now wondering if I can fit another bed in your dorm room so I can keep an eye on you."

Karensa put her arm around her mother and kissed her cheek. "Gosh, I'm going to miss you, Mom. I'll miss Dad, too, of course. I don't know how I'm going to get through life without my church youth group. We've grown up together, and it's like leaving other family members behind."

"You'll just have to find a new church here in Houston, honey. Since you'll be in the 'museum district', you can probably find a beautiful church to attend. I know you don't care about beauty—that it's the congregation that matters— but it would be nice to go to church in an architectural masterpiece. I'll just pray that you find the right church home, away from home."

A small slip of a girl walked up to them, her posture confident and proud. When she reached them she shook the mother's hand and then stood on tip-toes to hug Karensa. The difference in their height was amusing.

"Hey there! My name's Collette and I'm a junior here at Rice and I'll be your guide for the day. I want to show you how beautiful our campus is, the organizations you can become involved in, and introduce you to some of the freshmen currently living in the dorms. Now, where would you like to begin?"

The tour lasted the entire day. Both of them were pleasantly worn out when they thanked Collette and hugged her goodbye.

"See you in a few months, Ren!" Collette flashed her dimples before she turned to bounce away.

Karensa shook her head. "Ren? I was afraid to ask, but I'd bet ten bucks she's a cheerleader."

Beth chuckled, but it didn't reach her eyes. "Oh, honey, this is such a lovely campus and I envy you, getting to go to school here. But I sure am going to miss you!" She hit the keyless entry button of the car. For just a moment, Karensa looked pensive as she buckled her seatbelt.

"Yep, I'm going to miss you, too, Mom. But your little girl's all grown up now. It's time to head out into that big old world—"

"All grown up, huh? Oh, baby girl, when you truly *are* grown up, you'll realize that seventeen years is far from being an adult, but it's a start!" She laughed as she leaned across the console to hug her only daughter. "What do you say we stop by Red Lobster to celebrate your first step into adulthood, hmm?"

Karensa chuckled, "Okay, whatever, Mommy."

"Oh, so that's the way it's going to be, huh? Okay, just for that, I'm listening to my Milli Vanilli CD and I'm going to crank that puppy up!"

"Oh, no, Mom, please! I'll do anything you ask, just don't do that to me, I'm begging you. Hey, I'll even listen to The Bangles if I have to. Anything but the Phony Balognies!"

"What about a compromise, kiddo? How about we listen to Adele? We both like her."

"See? You're just the coolest mom, ever!"

"Don't you forget it, either, Sistah!"

"Sistah? Oh, that's like, saWeet, dude!"

"Okay, okay, I have to stop before I get nauseated with teenalogue!" Karensa groaned as her mother laughed.

"Okay, cheddar-cheese biscuits here we come!"

After Beth paid the bill, they walked to the front of the building kidding about needing to unbutton their pants.

"Next time we go to Red Lobster I'm wearing a dress with lots of room. Oh, I just love their food!"

Karensa held the door open for her mother. Beth groaned when she saw it had not only started to rain while they ate, but it had become a torrential downpour.

"It never fails, does it, kiddo? But if you hadn't had that piece of cake ..."

"Oh, Mom, are you going to try to act as if that chocolate-chip lava cookie wasn't worth a few raindrops?"

"Honey, this is more than a few raindrops. But you're right, that dessert would be worth going down with the Titanic!"

They ran the last few feet to the car, threw themselves inside and laughed with the joy of being together, having a good day, and enjoying a wonderful dinner. Life was good, even if it was wet.

Eyeing the traffic swarming along the expressway, calculating a maneuver that would allow them to slide smoothly in and blend with the rush hour traffic, Beth allowed a chuckle. "We might not be sinking with the Titanic over that dessert, but we're being flung into the last lap at NASCAR. Remind me again just how good that chocolate-chip lava cookie was, Honey."

Beth saw a break in the line of rushing traffic and pressed the accelerator to join the other commuters, all the while glancing at her rearview mirror to make sure she had plenty of room.

"It was, without a doubt, the absolutely bestest dessert in the entire ..."

What had been a three-car gap in traffic was cut in half by a red Hummer that was closing the gap with lightning speed.

Beth knew it was going to happen before the Hummer reached them. She threw her arm in front of her daughter, as if to forcefully protect her from the nightmare force barreling toward them much faster than the 55 mph speed limit allowed.

"Oh, my God ..."

"Mom? What's wrong? What is ..."

Beth looked into the eyes of the young woman behind the wheel of the Hummer. Her face had time to register the shock and the fact that she hadn't even seen the car she was about to decimate until the second she glanced up from texting on her cell phone.

Just before impact, Karensa heard the scream of the Hummer's tires on the wet pavement, clutched her mother's hand pressing against her chest, and whispered, "Mom?"

Inside their car, the world blurred as everything around the mother and daughter spun past in dizzying circles. The blow from the Hummer threw the car into the guardrail, back into the line of traffic, sending it flying into the side of a car driven by man out of town, causing it to fishtail into the path of an eighteen-wheeler. The last thing Beth and

Karensa heard were the squall of massive air brakes that failed to stop the mammoth truck's momentum.

Beth woke up in the hospital. Both legs were in traction and her left arm was held in place with what felt like a massive cast. She touched her forehead to find a bulbous, throbbing knot beneath bandages. The second she flinched from the painful touch, *Karensa*!

"Hey! Help! Nurse? Somebody, please!" She thought that her strident cries would bring half the staff but if anyone even heard her, they weren't responding fast enough. Her only thought was her daughter.

The nurse caught her trying to reach the traction device to free her legs.

"Whoa, whoa, whoa there, little lady. You can't get out of bed!"

"Karensa! My daughter! Where is she? I have to go see her now!"

"Beth, Honey, you can't get out of bed for any reason right now. You've been in a car wreck and have been injured ..."

"I know all that! The knot on my head didn't cause amnesia. I want to know about Karensa. I have to know if she's alright. I have to know ... Oh, God, is she dead?"

The nurse pressed her patient back against the pillows and talked as she smoothed the sheets.

"Karensa is not dead, Beth. She was pretty banged up in the accident, too. They put her in ICU to keep a close eye on her. Her injuries were more severe than yours."

"How much worse is she? Please, please, you have to tell me."

"Beth, your daughter isn't one of my patients and I don't have a report on her, so I can't answer your question. What I can do, however, is put in a call for Karensa's doctor to come talk to you now that you're finally awake."

"Finally?"

The nurse gently patted one of the legs in a cast, as if Beth could feel it and take comfort. "You've been unconscious for three days."

"Three days? Oh, Lord, what all has happened while I was out? Do you know where my husband is? Will you hand me the phone, please? I have to find someone to tell me what's going on!"

"Beth, you need to calm down a little." She pulled a syringe from her pocket, removed the cap and inserted the needle into the IV line. "This will just help you relax until I can get your family and Karensa's doctor in here to talk with you."

"No! I don't want a shot! I want to know what's going on with my daughter! I want to…"

Beth didn't see the expression of pity on the young nurse's face because she'd gone to sleep.

Their voices seemed to come from some sort of deep tunnel. Beth opened her eyes to see figures standing around her, surrounded with fog and murmuring in a language she didn't understand. It took nearly twenty minutes for her to become fully conscious from the aftereffects of the sedative she'd been given two hours earlier. The first voice she recognized was Mac's.

"Honey, can you hear me? Beth? You awake yet, Sweetheart? We need to talk to you."

Beth groaned and tried to turn over, away from the intrusion but the leg casts wouldn't allow movement.

Casts. My legs. I've been hurt. The wreck. Where was I? When did it happen? Who was …

"Karensa!"

Mac sighed, then smiled. Even in her medicated state, Beth recognized the fake "everything's going to be alright" smile. You get to know a person, their voice, their step, the mannerisms, well after twenty years of marriage. The smile might have been phony, but the red-rimmed eyes and the bruise-colored circles under his eyes were all too real.

The doctor stepped closer to the bed but Mac held up his hand to stop him. Without taking his eyes off his wife's face he spoke in a husky voice.

"Karensa's in ICU and she's not doing very well, Honey. You both were hurt very badly in that wreck but her injuries were more extensive."

Beth's eyes welled and her voice was faint, hushed. "How bad is she, Mac?"

Dr. Anderson again stepped forward, this time refusing to be dissuaded by his patient's father.

"I'm James Anderson, trauma surgeon, and just one of your daughter's many doctors. I hate to intrude but you need to hear this from a medical point of view. Afterward, if you have no further questions, I'll leave you fine people alone to come to grips with this."

His voice brooked no argument and was authoritative but also held enough compassion to make bad news a bit more bearable. Beth looked at Mac who nodded his head, then turned her gaze back to the doctor.

"From the police report and what we saw of Karensa's injuries, we've put together a logistical timeline of events. When Ms. Vonn struck your vehicle ..."

"That's her, the girl who nearly murdered us because she simply couldn't wait to send a text? The girl who cared more for her next message than she did the lives she was about to take out?"

Mac laid his hand on his wife's shoulder.

"No! I won't calm down and I know that's what you're trying to get me to do, Mac. I saw her face the minute she looked up from her phone, when she realized she was about to ..."

"Beth. Please. Let that go for now ..."

"Let it go? Let it go! No, I will not let it go, Mac! I want that girl arrested for attempted murder, or something! I want her ..."

Dr. Anderson's response was spoken softly but Beth heard him clearly, "Stacy Vonn died at the scene. A gentleman in another car, in town on a business trip and on his way home, was killed. The one seemingly immovable object, the tractor-trailer rig, flipped onto its side and caught fire. The driver was pinned inside and no one could reach him in time. Mrs. Wilson, you and Karensa were the only survivors of this terrible tragedy and I'm still trying to figure out how that happened."

Beth remembered the smooth, yet unlined face of the young woman staring back at her in horror and began to sob. Mac sat on the edge of her bed, trying to find a place to touch her that wouldn't cause pain, just so he could offer comfort. He'd had three days to work through this and that wasn't long enough; for Beth it had just happened.

The doctor gave her time to cry until she was reduced to sniffles before he continued. "Though I'm not a CSI like on one of those popular TV shows, I can envision the actions inside your car. Both you and Karensa were inside a whirlwind. It would be the equivalent to being trapped inside an industrial washing machine. The breaks you have in your bones are clean, even breaks and will heal quickly, though not, I'm sure, quickly enough for you. Your right leg has two breaks in the femur and one in the tibia. The left leg is broken in four places. Your arm is broken and is in a cast *and* a brace because your shoulder was twisted out of the socket and the rotator cuff was torn so badly it has to be kept totally immobilized for a few weeks. You're going to have a rough and bumpy road ahead but you *will* heal, in your own time."

"And Karensa?"

Dr. Anderson pulled a chair from the side of the room and sank slowly into it. Beth's eyes followed his every move.

"Now, Karensa ..." The sigh came from deep within. "Karensa was hurt very badly. The passenger side of the car was the side that hit the guardrail with all the force a speeding Hummer could put forth. Karensa's door was shoved inward, into her body which, in response, twisted around on its spine. With each repeated assault from different vehicles after that, more and more of her body was broken."

"Her head?"

"Strangely enough, that was the only part of her body that didn't have a mark on it."

"So there's no brain damage? Once she gets well, oh, I know that's going to take a long time but, once she heals, she can ..."

Her words ground to a halt when she saw her husband's head lower. His breathing became ragged as the doctor answered her unasked question.

"Beth, we're not sure Karensa will survive. The injuries are just so severe and medicine can only do so much ..."

"Nooooooo! She's going to be okay! You said yourself that she had no head injuries, Dr. Anderson!"

"Head injuries are not the only thing to take a life, Beth. Karensa lost a lot of blood, so there still may be brain damage due to that. In fact, it's most likely the case. Her liver was torn and half of it had to be removed, along with her spleen, a kidney and ..."

Mac groaned, "And all her reproductive organs had to be taken."

Beth sputtered, "I don't care! I don't care if she never has children. I know she wanted a houseful but I don't care if she never has one single child as long as she lives! Dr. Anderson, what happens next? What do we have to do to save our girl?"

"Her back is broken in so many places it'd take a hardware store to furnish enough plates and screws to put her back together. Even with that, she'll never walk again, that is, if she has no brain damage. All the plates and screws could do is put her back in one piece. Because of the extent of her injuries, all we're doing now is keeping her comfortable, waiting for you to wake up and give you time to discuss this with Mac."

"Discuss what? What's there to talk about? Do everything you can to fix her, get her back as close as she used to be and we'll take care of the rest. I can exercise her legs and arms after we take her home. I'll help her to move, to walk, again. You evidently underestimate the power of a mother's love, Doctor."

Mac put an arm across Beth's stomach and looked into her face, trying to impart some sort of warning about what was coming next.

"Mrs. Wilson, I've spoken to your husband. I've taken him in to see Karensa and he understands that ..."

Beth pushed Mac's arm away. "You understand what, Mac? Just what is it you know, that I don't?"

Mac couldn't speak for sobbing. Dr. Anderson replied for him.

"We suggest that you let her go. If you wish, we can discuss organ donation but ..."

Her scream could be heard at the other end of the hallway. Mac held her then, crying with her as she kept gasping, "No, no, no, no!"

"Honey, Karensa is gone. Our little girl isn't there anymore. We *have* to let her go."

"Get out of here, both of you! GET OUT!"

A nurse in the room injected the contents of a large syringe into the tubing of Beth's IV. The mother's hoarse screams subsided within seconds.

The next twenty-four hours passed in a drugged haze for Beth. Each time she awoke from her medicated slumber, she began to sob and pray. She then felt as if she'd run out of tears, but she still had an abundant supply of prayers left to offer. Once she calmed down to converse with God, the nurse stopped injecting sedatives.

Beth allowed Mac to come back into the room the next day. She realized she wasn't angry with him, she was just disappointed.

"Mac, when you needed God the most, you didn't reach out; you just gave up. God can do this. I have faith that He can and I'd like for you to be beside me when it happens. We have a daughter who needs to get well, finish school and live her life. If we both believe, really believe, it *can* happen."

He hugged her. "I just needed you to wake up and remind me what an idiot I am, Beth." He chuckled. "Okay, we'll turn it over to Him. It's for sure we can't fix Karensa, but He can."

A week later the nurse came into Beth's room and said she was going on a field trip. Beth laughed, "How can I go anywhere? I can't even get out of this bed."

"We're going to take you, bed and all, on this trip. Hang onto your sheets, 'cause here we go!"

People stepped out of the elevator to allow the nurses to push the metal-framed bed inside. Three floors down they got off. Beth saw the sign for ICU and started to smile through a new influx of tears. Her husband moved to the other side of Karensa's bed when he saw them wheeling his wife into the ICU. His face was wreathed in the kind of smile reserved for Christmas.

The beautiful young woman who Beth had brought into the world a short seventeen years before, the girl who was pronounced to be little more than an organ donor, called out, "Mom? Oh, Mom!"

Beth ached to jump out of her own hospital bed so she could gather her daughter in a tight hug. She wanted to hold her and never let her go again. The nurses maneuvered the beds close enough so that a mother could reach out and hold her only daughter's hand.

They talked for over an hour, about the accident, about their injuries, about the lives that had been lost, about how life could be gone in an instant. As their energy drained away, they talked about how much they loved each other, how much their family meant to them and how much God surely loved them to save them when all else had been lost.

"Mom, I'll be in surgery for most of tomorrow. Have you heard? They're going to put a bunch of plates and screws in my back!"

Beth smiled at Mac and he saw the fear in her face. "Yep, Dr. Anderson said ..."

They heard Dr. Anderson's voice before he reached the room and he sounded like a different man than the one who had brought a wrecking ball into Beth Wilson's life just a few days before.

"I said that I'd found just the hardware store that had enough supplies to fix up this young lady. I have to hand it to you, Mom, you showed me I was wrong."

"It wasn't me that prove you were wrong; it was God."

"Well, I certainly won't argue with Him and I've never been happier to be mistaken in my life."

The surgery lasted eleven hours and the rehab lasted six months. Karensa will graduate high school a year later than she would have before the accident, but everyone is just happy she's around to graduate at all. The cap and gown ceremony will be nice but this weekend will her first formal celebration of her return to life. She bought the most beautiful prom dress in the store and she looks gorgeous in red.

"Mom, I think I've changed my mind about my major for college. I think I want to be an orthopedic surgeon when I grow up. After all, look what great work they did on me!"

Avalanche!

"What color would you call that sky?"

"Uh ... blue?"

Ron laughed. "What imagery! What descriptive phrases! No wonder you're a writer!"

Simon curled his lip and did a hip shake, "Well thank ya, thank ya vury much!"

"Yeah, like I said, good thing you're a writer because you do a lousy John Wayne impersonation."

"John Wayne? Wow, I must be worse than I realized. If you can't recognize that as an Elvis impression from a hundred yards you're deaf, dumb and ...wait, you *are* dumb. Mystery solved!"

Ron shook his head sadly. "Are you going to ski or what? Let's forget the fact that you have no future in stand-up comedy and hit the slopes."

Simon clapped his best friend's back. "I know you're in a hurry to hit the Bunny Slope but how 'bout you let us grown-ups ski first?"

Ron lifted his pole and said, "I'll have you to know that I won a medal in skiing."

"Yeah, I know. I watched you stick a pin through a lid off a jelly jar and pin it on yourself." He put his hand over his heart. "It was a proud moment for all of us that know you for the champion athlete that you are."

"We'll see just who beats who, or it is whom, to the bottom first, Si!"

"Ah, but it's not the speed at which we ski, but the view of the sky, the snow and the babes on the way down the mountain. By the way, I'll be seeing all of that before you because I'm not only faster, I'm better. The only way you'll pass me is if you fall and slide by on your butt or rolling like the big old snowball you already are."

"Okay, okay, go ahead and make fun of me. I'll show you who survives this war!"

Simon walked toward the ski supply shop. "Well, hold up there, Pilgrim. I have to go buy a locating beacon before we go into battle."

"You really going to buy one of those? We've never used them before. Why today?"

He shrugged. "I don't know; just seems like a good idea for some reason. They can't be too expensive, right? Besides, I think I might need one, hanging around with you. There's no telling where you'll wind up getting us stuck one of these days."

Ron scowled good-naturedly. "I've never gotten you 'stuck' that you didn't have fun, Si! But go ahead, waste your money. I'll meet you outside."

Talking to the salesman, Simon realized the PLB devices were a little more expensive than he'd first thought they would be. He'd considered buying one for Ron, too, but he couldn't afford it. He knew Ron's money was also tight, so they'd only have the one device. The ski trip had been a graduation gift from their parents. They both had saved their own money for extras, but Ron had used most of his money to help his mom pay for his dad's funeral.

Ron's father had passed away a month before this trip. At first, Ron said he didn't want to go skiing, after all. But the tickets were nonrefundable and his mother had told him how happy his father had been to give his son this trip as a gift and how hurt he'd be if Ron didn't take it. "Go have fun for your dad, honey. If he'd been here, he might've gone with you boys, just to show you how to do it right." She'd smiled at the thought.

So here they were in the beautiful mountains, ready for some serious, yet fun, skiing. Though nothing would erase the loss of Mr. Thomas, three days playing on snow that sparkled like diamonds in the glistening sunshine made even heartbroken men smile at times. They'd even met a couple of pretty ladies who, like them, were slaloming as a celebration of one of life's accomplishments. Both of them started college the next semester and, crazy enough, it was within driving distance of the college Simon and Ron were attending. That is, if all parties were interested in seeing each other again. So far, it seemed they were. The four young people had been inseparable since checking in at the same time. The only reason they weren't with the men today is the women were vastly inexperienced on the slopes and had decided they needed lessons before they joined their new friends on "the big people hills".

"Already got them skis on, ready to rock 'n roll, huh Ron?" He patted his friend's shoulder, then playfully shoved him a couple of times, even acting like he was going to yank Ron's jacket off.

Ron jerked away, letting Simon know he wasn't up to goofing off. "Hey, ain't that why we came out here? C'mon Si, let's go have a good time for my dad!" His smile was a bit melancholy but Simon could tell Ron was trying hard to have a good time.

Si plastered a big smile on his own face and punched his buddy's shoulder. "Okay, last one to reach the bottom has to unload the car all by yourself, Ron, when we get home. Last chance to chicken out!"

"The only laying eggs *and* unloading the car is you, Mr. Davis!"

Simon made a big production of turning on the PLB he'd just bought. "Uh-huh. The only way you'll be able to keep up with me, Ronald, is by tracking this!" With the last syllable he pushed off and over the decline.

"Hey! No fair, you big cheat!" Ron was mere seconds behind his pal.

It was later in the day than many skiers liked to run so Ron and Si had the slope mostly to themselves, just the way they liked it. They both felt it was more peaceful, and somehow more freeing, when no one else was around. It was also the most dangerous time; a fact that made it stimulating and exciting to the two young men.

Ron had skied within a few feet of Simon, catching up with him on the downward slope. They were both laughing, shouting playful insults to each other when they heard the first rumble. By the time they heard the second rumble, they began to feel it beneath their skis. Both of their faces registered the shocked terror. Then they simultaneously screamed one word, "Avalanche!"

Simon and Ron dug their poles into the snow, each stab more rapid and frantic than the one before, racing with an enemy that could prove deadly if it caught them.

Hardened balls of snow began pelting them, slapping at their backs, hammering their heads, threatening to knock their legs from beneath them. The faster they slalomed, the faster the snow barreled down upon them.

As if one person, both turned to look back at the same time. It was their undoing. Either the sight of tons of snow hurtling toward them was so unsettling they fell, or the ground shifted in such a way it caused them both to go down. Though they struggled to pull free, each man was covered by snow within seconds.

Ron had no idea how long he'd been knocked out. He only knew that he awoke to a nightmare of gargantuan proportions. He was encased in a tomb of ice and snow so profound, all he could see was darkness. Somehow his movements, the way he landed, the grace of God, *something* had created an air pocket. A preciously small air pocket to be sure, but Ron was saying prayers of gratitude for that one huge blessing.

His next thought was of Simon, his best friend since fifth grade. He drew in as deep a breath as possible and shouted out his friend's name. Shouted? It sounded more like a muffled whimper, which is exactly what it was. No human ear could have ever heard that.

He worked feverishly to move his head, his arms, or his hands. His brain told his feet to kick, search for a way to break through. No matter how hard he struggled, Ron was unable to successfully move even one finger. He felt his heartbeat at his temple and it seemed to be speeding up with each new revelation of just how doomed he truly was.

The pocket of air seemed to be shrinking, growing smaller with each frantic gasp of air Ron pulled into his lungs.

I need to slow down and focus on nice, even, slow breaths. I won't last long if I keep gulping air like a fish out of water. Oh, God, who am I kidding? If I had any sense, I'd breathe harder, faster, use up what little oxygen I have as fast as possible and get this over with. All I'm doing is prolonging the inevitable.

Ron had never experienced a darkness, a void, as complete as this. His mind became so terrified he started to long for death just to escape the horror of it all. It wasn't long before the fear began to subside because his brain was being starved of oxygen. With his last conscious thought, he realized it wasn't going to be so bad, after all, because it was just like going to sleep. He would simply doze off and wake up on the other side of Heaven. He smiled, thinking of his father there waiting for him.

Ron was angry when he was first awakened from unconsciousness. His deprived brain was hallucinating; so determined to live, his brain was creating voices. This irritated Ron who had been blissfully surrendering to death. The closer he reached escaping this world's problems, the louder the voices seemed to become.

When he felt vibrations near his body, he began to cry, not from relief but from being denied.

Dad! I'm so sorry, Dad. I almost …

A blast of air washed over his face then he heard a loud roar of triumph, strong in the fading sunset. It took him a few seconds to open his eyes. He had to squint against the glare of torches and flashlights. So many hands scraped and brushed the hard-packed snow from around his body that he couldn't see the sky above him.

"Careful people! He's probably got broken bones. We don't want to injure him further by rushing. Sir? Sir, can you hear me? Sir, are you Simon Davis?"

Simon!

"No, my name's Ron Thomas. My buddy's name is Simon. He was with me. Where is he?"

"Ron? But the signal we got was from a PBL that a Simon Davis bought. We found it in your jacket pocket, sir."

"In my pocket? No, that can't be right. Si stopped by the gift shop to buy one and he ..." Ron now remembered Simon horse-playing just before he tipped his skis and went over the precipice—first one out of the starting gate. He must have slipped the PLB device into Ron's pocket then. "He was acting silly, goofing around, and he must have sneaked that thing in my pocket. But, where is he? Where's Simon?"

They called in more volunteers, even members of the ski patrol who had been off duty, but it still took them another three hours to find Si's body. He'd managed to stay on his feet a little longer than Ron before getting caught by the avalanche. Had he kept the locating beacon, it would've been Ron's body they dug out of the snow.

* * *

Starting college without Simon was just as depressing as Ron thought it would be. He studied hard trying to rid his mind of what had happened, but it didn't work. He kept thinking it should've been him who died that day on the slope. Then Kathy called him.

Kathy Tramer had been the young woman who Simon had been spending time with that weekend at the ski lodge. When she first called Ron she wanted to talk about Simon, to talk about the brief time she'd spent with the handsome young man. Over the months, their shared affection for Simon became affection for each other.

Two years after the avalanche, Ron Thomas and Kathy Tramer were married. The best man was there only in spirit. When their first son was born, they named him Simon Thomas.

They have started a small box of keepsakes that will grow larger over the years. The first thing that went into that box was a Personal Locating Beacon and Ron will tell his son it was the first gift he received-from his uncle Simon.

The War at Home

She was holding the refrigerator door open, staring into it as if the answer to world peace lay somewhere on the wire shelves. Her head was cocked sideways, one hand on her hip, the instep of her right foot resting on the calf of her left leg. She didn't hear his soft step behind her, just as he'd hoped she wouldn't. He stepped behind her, mere inches from her back, yet she never felt his presence. He grinned in anticipation of what was coming next.

"That's the problem with these things; you have to watch them every second. You just never know when they'll do something silly."

She jerked around, nearly toppling to the floor due to the stance she had taken, the scream dying on her lips when she saw who it was.

"Christopher! Oh honey, it *is* you! Oh God, my Christopher!"

"Of course it's me, Mom. Who else named Christopher do you think would be stalking you in your own kitchen?"

"Honey, oh honey! I didn't know you were coming home! Oh lord, this is wonderful! When did you get home? How long can you stay? You don't have to go back, do you? What did you decided to do about re-upping?"

"Whoa, slow down there, Mom! Catch your breath and give me a chance to catch mine. For a lady who hasn't seen her son in nearly a year you ask an awful lot of questions."

Kristen wrapped her arms around her son and cried buckets of happy tears. They stood that way for a long time, holding each other, rocking back and forth, as they had before he'd shipped out to Afghanistan. The only difference this time would be that he wouldn't be going into a war zone when she let him go.

Without taking her arms away, she leaned back and smiled through her tears. "So what do you want for dinner, my sweet soldier boy?"

"I want to take my poor ol' crippled mother out to eat."

She finally let him go, only to poke him lightly in the stomach. "Poor ol' crippled mother, huh? She just might be too sick and tired to cook dinner for you ever again, after that remark."

Chris chuckled. "We both know that's not true. My poor ol' ma would always cook for me."

Kristen kissed his face and smiled. "You're right, you spoiled little brat, you. Now, where are you taking me?"

"How about you name the place, Mom? Don't worry about the price, either. Nothing's too good for my poor old mother."

Her look of mock disapproval didn't stop his laughter. "Honey, I don't care where we go. My baby boy is home; that's all I care about!"

"Now if you go around calling me your baby boy in public, I may just go get you a take-out pizza."

She saluted him and said, "Sir, yes sir!"

Chris reached over and messed up her hair while she tried to back away. "Go on, change clothes, put on some lipstick. I plan on taking you to the Avalon for the best steak in town."

Kristen started shaking her head. "Oh no, honey, that's way too expensive. I don't mind that pizza you talked about. Yeah, that's what we'll do. I'll comb my hair and we'll go grab a pizza."

"Mom, unless you want to be embarrassed wearing your holey jeans and ratty tennis shoes at the Avalon, you might want to really change. I was joking about you choosing where we go. I've already made reservations so get a move on!"

The bad thing about a small town is that everyone knows everyone else. The good thing about a small town is everyone knows everyone else. Within minutes of being seated at their table, Kristen and Christopher were deluged with friends wanting to hug, kiss, and just generally welcome home their hometown hero.

"Hey, Chris, good to see you, son!"

"So good to have you back home where you belong, Christopher."

"It seems like it's been years since we've seen you, son."

"Glad to have you back home, safe and sound."

"We've been praying for you and the rest of our troops, Chris."

"Praise be to God for bringing you back home to Mama's cooking. Right, Chris?"

No matter how many people stopped by the table, Christopher stood up for each person who wanted to shake hands or give him a hug. His food grew cold and he began to look tired, but he never lost that winning smile. Kristen was proud of her boy. Everyone who knew them had always told her what a wonderful job she'd done raising him alone after his father lost his life on the job, during a routine traffic stop over fifteen years before.

Emily, their waitress, came by with their check. "How was everything? Chris, how long are you going to be home? It sure is good to see you again."

As she was handing the check to the young man, John, the owner of Avalon, walked by and took it from her. "That'll be on the house tonight, Mr. Johnson."

Chris smiled and reached for the check. "Oh sir, that's very kind of you, but really, I—"

"Now, Chris, what kind of ungrateful man would I be to let one of our fine upstanding soldiers pay for his meal?"

"Sir, I appreciate the thought, but I promised Mom here that I'd take her out to eat and—"

"And that's exactly what you did, Chris. Now let me show you my gratitude and allow me to do this one small thing."

Emily stood by the table, looking at the check as she chewed on her lip. John said, "Yes, Emily? Is something wrong?"

"Uh, well, I, uh, just had written something on there and, uh ..."

Her pretty petite face turned a lovely shade of pink as John turned the check over and read what it said.

"Chris, party tomorrow night for you. Call me: 555-2020. Emily. Well, it would appear our little Miss Emily here is asking you out, Chris."

Kristen smiled at the young woman with an understanding half-smile. "Well, Emily, that wasn't embarrassing at all, was it?"

It was John's turn to blush. "Oh, dear, I'm so sorry, Em. I didn't mean to do that."

Chris stood up, held out his hand and said, "Emily, I'd love to go to the party with you. Would you please write your number on my hand?"

With cheeks flaming, Emily wrote her number then scrambled to escape her humiliation. John shook Chris' hand before making his own hasty retreat.

Chris laughed. "Well, do we know how to clear a room or what, Mom?"

He left a large tip then put his arm around his mother's shoulders as they left the restaurant.

While so many people had been welcoming her son home, Kristen had surreptitiously held her cell phone under the table and texted a few key people. In the space of the time that it took to order, eat and speak to several people, a celebration had been put together.

Chris looked up and down his old neighborhood streets, his eyebrows knitted together. "Mom, I know Laneford is a small town, not populated with wild people that party hearty, but it's only 8 p.m. on Friday night. Where is everyone? Sheesh. Everyone's porch lights are off; even the inside lights are off. This is weird. Is there some sort of thing going on that I don't know about, like a carnival or a craft fair at the school?"

Kristen shook her head as she wrapped her arms around one of his. "No, not that I know of, honey. But I don't read the newspaper very often so there could be some big shindig going on I don't know about."

He grinned at her, then chuckled out loud. "Shindig? What generation are you from, Grandma Moses?"

She was laughing so hard she couldn't fit the key into the lock. The more she tried, the harder she laughed until she dropped it.

"Here Mom, let me do this. How much did you drink at dinner, anyway?"

"Oh, listen to you! I drank my usual two glasses of iced tea, just like you did."

He turned the knob and pushed the door open. "Well, don't let them call me as a witness because I'd have to say I think it was something other than tea—"

"Surprise!!" Chris jerked backwards, stepping on his mother's toes as he did so. He held his arms rigid, his fingers pressed together to form a slicing surface, his knees were bent and his back was ramrod straight. When it registered it was his neighbors shouting a cheer, he released his pent-up breath slowly. He bent over from his waist and rested his hands on his knees, head hung low and inhaling deeply. Even though his brain now realized it wasn't a fight or flight situation, it would take longer for the adrenaline to stop rushing through his veins.

Kristen limped over to him to put an arm around him. "Oh baby, I'm so sorry. It never occurred to us how you'd react. I'm an idiot! Oh Chris, if we'd known ..."

He stood up, kissed his mother's cheek and turned a smile to the assembled family and friends gathered around. "No, I'm sorry, Mom. I didn't know I'd react like that and embarrass you. Please, let's just try to act like it never happened, okay?"

"Chris, I just wanted to surprise you."

He laughed out loud. "Well, you certainly did that! Mission accomplished! Aw, c'mon Mom, you got this together in lightning speed so let's have some fun. What is it your generation might say? Oh, yeah, 'Let's party like it's 1999!' Woot woot!"

"Cute, Chris, very cute. Now go find someone else to irritate." Her loving smile belied the words that came out. Her son grinned and said, "Oh, you know you love me!"

Tears slid down her cheeks. "Oh baby boy, more than my own life. Now, go away and leave me alone. This is for you, so have fun!"

Chris scanned all the familiar faces, grinned at some, made comments to others, shook his head in mock pity at a few former fellow football players as they tried to dance and then he saw her. Emily was on the far side of the room, being held prisoner by Reverend Thacker; a good man who didn't know when to stop talking. Emily was nodding, smiling, and glancing at Chris a few times as he made his way through the crowd. He heard her sigh of relief when he reached her side.

"Preacher Thacker! Wow, it's been a long, long time! How have you been, sir?"

"Chris!" He pulled the young man into a bear hug that threatened to squeeze the air from Chris' lungs. "It's so, so good to see you, son! Why, my ol' heart just about stopped beating when I got that call tonight that you were home, safe, all in one piece. You know what I mean there, Chris." Shaking his head Reverend Thacker laid his arm around Chris' shoulders. "We got too many boys coming home in boxes, Chris. Too many coming home with pieces missing, their minds messed up and their hearts broken by what they saw, what they had to do *over there*."

The smile slid from Chris' face but he kept his eyes on the minister's face, waiting for him to fully realize that he was saying these things to one of those very same young men whose fate he was bemoaning. Evidently, it had to be more obvious for the preacher to understand. He took a deep breath, ready to launch into a new diatribe on the horrors of war when Emily stepped in to save him.

"Excuse me, Reverend Thacker, but my favorite song is playing and Chris promised me he'd dance with me when it played. Please, forgive me. Come on, Chris, you promised!" She tugged at his arm and Chris smiled an apology to the minister.

"Sorry, sir, a promise is a promise."

Reverend Thacker smiled back and said, "It sure is, Chris, and you never want to break a promise to a sweet young lady. You kids go on; have a good time. We'll talk later." He turned around, "Hey, Mrs. Battenfield! I've been looking for you. We need to talk about that ladies' auction you're organizing ..."

Chris and Emily walked to the middle of the dancers and shuffled their feet, somewhat in rhythm to the music. "Em, when did I promise I'd dance with you to this song?"

"You didn't."

"Oookay, so what's the name of this song? Who sings it?"

"I have no idea."

"You lied to a man of the cloth to get away from him?"

"Chris, I would have given him my first born child when I have one to get away from him."

He hugged Emily to him, picked her up, and twirled her around a few times. "You know, Emily, I think I like you."

She laid her head at the center of his chest and grinned.

They swayed back and forth until the end of the song then Chris leaned back to look into her face.

"So, Emily, where is this party going to be tomorrow night?"

"Down at the lake. As soon as Rick heard you were back, he started putting it together. You probably hadn't been home thirty minutes before he heard and started arranging everything."

As if on cue a voice from the front door was raised above all the noise of people talking and music playing to reach Chris' ear.

"The conquering hero has returned home victorious, I say! Sergeant Johnson, sir! Richard, AKA the Rickster, Harmon reporting for duty, sir!"

Chris hung onto Emily's hand as he crossed the room to greet his best friend. He stopped a couple of feet in front of him and looked his pal over from head to toe.

"Oh really? The Rickster, huh? And just who gave you that nickname, private? Oh, let me guess; you gave it to *yourself*! Yeah, ready for duty, are you, son? I highly doubt that but I'll give you the benefit of the doubt, just because that's the kind of guy I am. So, drop and give me twenty now, private!"

"Sergeant Johnson, sir! Because I was so grievously injured when I carried you on my back all those times we played football, especially when we played our rivals, I regret I am unable to follow your orders. But as team leader, sir, you should show us that it can, indeed, be done. I mean, if our leader can't do it, how can he expect *us* to do it?"

Chris gave Emily's hand a light squeeze before letting it go. He then dropped and began doing push-ups. It wasn't long before people formed a circle around him to watch.

"One. Two. Three. Four. Five ..." By the time Chris reached fifty the crowd was shouting each number. He then stood up and everyone applauded. In the middle of the noise, his pal yelled, "Show off!" Then Rick stepped close enough for only Chris to hear him. "It's so good to have you back, bro. Don't you ever leave again. This place isn't the same without you, man."

Chris lightly punched him in the belly and laughed in embarrassment. "You're just saying that 'cause it's true, Rick. Now come on, enjoy the party."

"This is nice, Chris, but the one we'll have tomorrow night will be a real party."

His eyes narrowed and his brows drew lower. "Just what do you mean by a real party, Rick?"

"Oh man, you know—loud music. Hey, I even got somebody to DJ for free! Lots of chicks and kegs and kegs of beer."

Chris shook his head. "I was with you until you got to the word *kegs*. Rick, why not try one party without booze?

Just see how it goes? Man, I've seen too much legitimate drama complete with blood and guts to come home and see the same thing being done in the name of fun instead of freedom."

"Aw, man, what happened? Did you go to Afghanistan and go all holy on us, Chris? What kind of party would it be without booze?"

"Uh, a fun one where no one is hurt, angry or winds up behind bars?"

"Shoot, Chris, that's how we always measured how great a party it was!"

"Yeah, I know that. It was immature then and it's even more so now that we're adults."

"We're 22 years olds—barely adults. Anyway, it doesn't matter. There'll be booze there even if I don't bring in kegs. You know everyone brings their own. I can't believe you changed so much in a few months."

"And you'd never believe the stuff I've seen and done in those few months, either, Rick. We'll still have the party but don't be shocked if I don't drink. I've discovered I don't have to soak it up to have fun, plus I don't feel like I've been hit by a Mack truck the next morning. Just let me know what time and I'll be there."

"You better be there, man, since this party's in your honor."

Chris pushed Rick's shoulder and chuckled. "In my honor, huh? Rick, man, you look for any excuse to party."

Rick grinned. "Ah, you know me so well! Well, I'm going to hit the road. This 'party' is too tame for my tastes; besides, I need to get the word out about the real party tomorrow night."

"Rick, don't invite any rough guys. I'm home to relax for a couple of weeks. I don't want to go to a party and have to fight because you let your mouth overload your brain again."

"Oh, that ain't a nice thing to say, Christopher. Shame on you!" A grin lit up his buddy's handsome face. "See you tomorrow, dude!"

* * *

Kristen called her boss the next morning to ask for the day off to spend with her son. To her delight, when Bob answered the phone he said, "I hope you're not trying to come to work today. Rumor has it that you have a young man there eating you out of house and home. Since I'm afraid it might be contagious, I'd rather you stay home and take care of that ravenous person before he attacks every food-based business in town. Have fun and we'll see you tomorrow!"

Mother and son spent their day doing unimportant things such as driving through town so Kristen could point out new buildings under construction, and accompanying Chris when he went by the high school to see his former football coach. She insisted Chris go with her to the grocery store so she'd be sure to pick up things he'd want. It was then that the day became overcast.

"I know it's still a few weeks away, but do you know how many friends you might invite for Easter dinner? I just want an idea so I'll know how large a ham to get."

He faced his window, seemingly so interested in the passing scenery that he didn't hear her question.

"Chris? Honey? How many people do ..."

"None, Mom. I won't be inviting any people over for Easter dinner because I won't be here."

Kristen was so surprised it took her a few seconds to respond. "But, what do you mean you won't be here, Chris?"

"I'll be back in Afghanistan, Mom."

She pulled the car to the curb and put the gearshift into park. "What are you talking about, Chris? You're out of the Marines, honey, so why would you be going back?"

Chris had a sad smile on his face as he looked at her, waiting for her to put it together for herself.

"Oh my God, you re-upped. Chris?" She began to slowly shake her head, then she shook it faster and faster until her son took her face in his hands.

"Mom, I had to. It's not over; it's not going to be over for a long time. They need all the help they can get. They need me."

"No Chris, no! I need you! This town needs you! You've been there twice now and you've given enough! Absolutely not! I won't allow this. I just won't let you go; that's all there is to it."

His smile was rueful. "Mom, I'm 22 years old so, legally, I don't need your permission. I know you're hurt, and mad, but they need me over there, Mom! And I can't be at peace if I don't go back to help them."

"Sweetheart, please don't leave us again. I'm so scared you won't come back next time."

"You're my mother, and I have aunts, uncles and cousins all over town and, man, I love my family with all my heart. But Mom, those guys over there are my brothers; they're my family, too. I can no more leave them in harm's way than I could leave you if someone were trying to kill you."

Kristen buried her face in her hands and sobbed. Chris reached into the glove box and grabbed a few napkins. He pressed them into her hands and pulled her as close to him as the center console would allow.

"Mom, please don't make this harder than is already is. I couldn't wait to get home, see you, spend time with my friends but I started dreading this moment the second my plane landed. Please tell me it's okay, Mom. Please tell me you're okay with this."

She blew her nose and then wiped her eyes. "Chris, I can't tell you that. I'm not okay with it because I love you and never want any harm to come to you. If I could, I'd go in your place and take anything that would hurt you so you'd never experience pain or fear. But I can't do that, either. All I can do is tell you that I'm so proud of you; that I'm amazed every day that God gave me a son like you. It's because you're so phenomenal that you want to go back to help. I'll never stop worrying but I'll also never stop praying so all I can do at this point is let you go and wait for you to come back home to me."

Chris kissed the top of her head and rubbed her back. "Death by chocolate."

She pulled back to look into his face. "What? What are you talking about?"

"You want to know what I want at the store, right? I want Death by Chocolate ice cream, two gallons of it!"

Laughing, she put the car in gear and they headed to the store.

* * *

After dinner of chicken alfredo, garlic bread and dessert of Death by Chocolate ice cream, Chris insisted on cleaning up the kitchen.

"Wow, I remember a day not too long ago that I couldn't bribe you into cleaning up."

"Sure you could've, Mom. You just didn't know the right stuff to bribe me with. But now that I'm grown I just realize that evolved men do their part in taking care of things around the house."

"Well Mr. Modern Man, what are your plans for the night? Are you going to take Emily up on her offer of a date?"

"Actually, I am, in a way. I'm going to meet her at the lake where a bunch of us are getting together later."

"Chris, the lake? Things have a habit of going bad out there lately. The cops are called to a fight or something just about every weekend."

"They won't be called out there this weekend, at least not because of us. I didn't want to say anything because it's sort of embarrassing but Rick is getting a bunch of our old friends together to well ... because of me. He's even gotten a DJ and the whole nine yards."

"Oh Chris, he's giving you a party because he's proud of you. That's so nice of him. Rick is a good boy but he can get a bit rowdy. I just hope everyone behaves themselves."

"I told him no kegs and he almost fainted. I suggested a party with no booze at all and he looked at me as if I'd grown another head or something. Then he started saying I've gotten all holy and religious on him, that I've changed."

Kristen was quiet, waiting for him to explain in his own way.

"It's not that I've gotten holy or something, Mom, it's just that I have changed. I tried to tell Rick that Afghanistan changes everyone who goes there. I'm not a bible-thumper but I do now believe with all my heart that there's something or someone out there, watching out for us. That doesn't mean we don't have to be afraid; it just means that it's okay to be afraid but you can have hope, too. Know what I mean? I sound silly, don't I? I'd never say any of this to Rick or the others because they'd think I'm a goody two-shoes now. I'm not. I'm still me, just with a different outlook on life."

She hugged her son then took the dish cloth out of his hand. "I think I understand, Chris, and I'm happy you finally understand there is more to us than this life. Now, go change; make yourself smell good for Emily."

"Aw, Mom!"

"And you might want to gargle twice since we had garlic bread."

She chuckled when he said, "Ah, but I didn't eat any because I know girls don't want to kiss a guy who stinks."

"That's my boy—planning ahead!"

There must have been thirty cars already parked next to the lake. Since it was only 8:00 Chris was sure there would be more people showing up as the night wore on.

Gee Rick, just how many people did you tell about this "little" party, anyway?

He hadn't gotten very far when he heard his best friend yell, "Hey, the man of the hour has arrived! C'mon Chris, I have a pile of sand here with your name written on it."

"Sure, Rick, just what I've always wanted—more sand."

"Oh, man, sorry Chris, I didn't even think about Afghanistan when I said that."

"Hey, buddy, not a problem. I was joking. So, where's *my* sandbox?"

Rick took his arm and led him over to a real wooden box that was used as a platform for the folding lawn chair. It had a banner on the back that said, "Reserved for Our Hero, Chris!"

"Aw, Rick, man, that's embarrassing! C'mon, take the banner off, will ya?"

Emily came bouncing up and grabbed Chris' hand. "Hey, how do you like the banner I put on the back of your chair? Pretty cool, huh?"

Rick raised his eyebrows at Emily's question. "Yeah Chris, what d'ya think about the sign Em made just for you?"

Chris smiled at Emily then turned to scowl at Rick. "Why Rick, I think it's cool. Thanks Em; that was very sweet of you."

Rick laughed and walked over to talk to the DJ. Soon the twilight night was filled with the sounds of different genres of music, from rap to country and everything in between.

Several times during the evening someone would offer Chris a beer or something stronger. He'd hold up his glass of cola and tell them he had to perform surgery the next morning so he was flying straight tonight. They all had a laugh about it and no one gave him any hassle about drinking after that.

The last few notes of "Amazing" by Bruno Mars was winding down. Chris and Emily were dancing to the slow tune just at the edge of the shadows. He was making her laugh and she was making him feel special; they were both falling in love. It would soon be midnight and Emily had just told him she'd have to leave soon.

"Summer is just around the corner so I don't want to get grounded before the school year is even over. Besides, if I got grounded and, say, some really cool guy wanted to go out with me ... Hey, who's that?"

Chris groaned when he recognized the rag tag group walking up the beach. Four of the roughest troublemakers in town looked as if they were bored and looking for something to break. Most likely, the laughter and music of a party they hadn't been invited to was what had their attention.

The troublemakers walked past Chris and Emily as they headed for the bonfire. The young couple saw the ax stuck in the back of one of the guy's belt. Emily looked at Chris and he shrugged to indicate he didn't know what was going on.

Rick approached the four guys but he was surrounded by at least ten other men. "What are you doing here, Ben? I don't think you, or any of your buddies here, were invited."

"Yeah, why is that, Rick? Why is it that you didn't tell us about this party? What, we ain't good enough for you guys?"

"This is a private bash, held for a friend of ours. You don't know him. We only invited people he knows."

"Oh yeah? I bet we know him. Hey, it's a small town; everybody knows everybody else. What's his name?"

Emily clutched at Chris' arm when he tried to walk toward the four thugs.

One of them started walking around and when he got to the back of the lawn chair and saw the banner, he laughed. "Hey, Ben, come look at this."

"What is it, Ted?"

One of the others walked over and read it out loud: "Reserved for our hero, Chris."

Ben turned to Rick with a snarl, "Well, ain't that just one of the sweetest darned things you ever heard, Devin? Gosh, that chokes me up."

The one named Devin stepped into the mix. "What kind of hero are we talking about here? Some kind of war hero? Those guys make me want to puke. They go to some foreign country and sit behind a desk, then tell all of us they were shot at and stuff. I bet this guy ain't nuttin' but a ..."

Chris pulled free of Emily's clutch and stood next to Devin. "He ain't nuttin' but a ... what, Devin?"

Ben moved closer to Devin and looked Chris over from head to toe. "Is it you, Johnson? You the big, bad war hero? You the one they're having this big hoorah for?"

"Yeah, that'd be me, alright. Why don't you guys just go on about your business and leave us alone? The party is just about over anyway. Let's just let everyone finish their drinks and clean up; then we'll call it a night. No harm, no foul."

"No harm, no foul, hmm? Who are you, Ghandi? Whatcha gonna do if we don't leave, G.I. Joe? You gonna use some of that kiiii rottie? You gonna pull some stealth moves like a ninja? Hey guys, we got us a ninja warrior here! What d'ya think about that?"

Ben drew his fist back and that's when Emily ran between the two men. Chris put his hands on her shoulders and pivoted around, moving her out of harm's way. As he was turned, Devin jerked a burning log from the fire and slammed it into Chris' back, hitting him square across the shoulder blades. The force of the blow knocked the young soldier to his knees.

Rick and others moved closer, their own fists pulled back, ready to jump into the fight when the next move froze everyone where they stood in shocked disbelief. Only in movies do unbelievable things like that happen.

Chris was still on his hands and knees when Ben stepped in front of him, swinging his arms above his head into a downward arc. Just as Chris' eyes met the other man's, Ben swung the ax down to embed it into the top of Chris' skull. Time seemed to stop, only to restart, when Emily screamed.

The two factions divided and scrambled in two different directions; the intended guests all ran to Chris, anxious to do anything possible to help; the party crashers ran back in the direction they had arrived. Some heard the roar of Devin's Charger's glass pack and he flung dirt and gravel in his hasty retreat.

Chris was lying on his side, eyes open and staring outward, into nothing. Rick kept assuring him, "You'll be okay, help is on the way. Hang in there, just hang in there, buddy."

Emily's tears fell on Chris' face as she leaned over him, finally telling him what she'd waiting all evening to say. "I love you, Chris Johnson. You hear me? Don't you dare leave me like this. I've waited years for you and I'm not giving up this easily and I won't let you, either." One of her friends tried to hug her but she was too distraught and pushed the girl gently away.

When the paramedics arrived on the scene they were also shocked; not only because of the injury but also because he was still breathing, and not having any difficulty doing so. They slipped a cervical collar around Chris' neck, eased him onto a backboard, then ran with him to the ambulance. The lights and siren were bouncing off the trees and hills, announcing the emergency before they even left the lake bank.

* * *

Kristen had just turned off her bedside lamp and was snuggling down into the sheets when the phone rang. At first she was confused, unable to understand the words through the wracking sobs coming over the phone line.

"Wait. Who is this? I'm sorry, but I can't understand you. Please, take a deep breath ..." Then her mother's intuition hit and she yelled into the phone. "Is it Chris? Did something happen to my son?"

"Yes ... oh, Mrs. Johnson ..."

"Emily? Emily, what happened? Where's Chris?"

"The ambulance ... hospital ... hurt bad ..."

"What happened? Emily, stop crying and tell me!!"

"... party ... Ben and Devin ... ax ..."

Kristen slammed the phone down and jumped out of bed. She picked it back up, dialed the police, all while pulling clothes over her head.

"Mrs. Johnson, I'm sorry I can't give you any information. All I know is that someone was hurt at the lake and an ambulance was dispatched. As to whether or not it is your son, and what those injuries might be, I have no idea at this time. I do know that the ambulance is transporting a patient to Laneford General Hospital and ...”

Kristen threw the phone on the bed, grabbed her purse and was fishing for her keys as she ran to her car. She arrived at the ambulance bay of the ER seconds after they had rushed their patient into the trauma bay. As she ran down the hall, she watched the double doors close behind the gurney. Just before she reached them, a police officer stepped in front of her.

“Ma’am, I’m sorry. You aren’t allowed to go in there.”

“You don’t understand. I believe that’s my son, Christopher Johnson, who has been hurt. I got a phone call from his girlfriend—”

“Mrs. Johnson, please speak to the nurse at the desk. She can answer more questions than I can and if it is your son, she’ll need to ask you questions, too.”

Beneath his breath, where no one but God could hear him, the officer prayed, *Please God, if that’s her boy, comfort her because she’d going to need your strength more than ever before. And no matter whose son that boy is, Lord, please place your hand upon him. In Jesus’ name I pray, Amen.*

“Mrs. Johnson? Is your son’s name Christopher Thomas Johnson, age 22?”

Kristen had thought it was impossible to shake more than she already was, but she was wrong. Here was confirmation that the patient in trauma was, without a doubt, her son. She forced herself to take deep, even breaths.

She stepped closer to the nurse. “Yes ma’am, that’s my son. Please, tell me what happened to him. Is he alright?”

“Ma’am I’m sorry but ...”

Everyone in the room stopped speaking when Kristen finally lost control. “If one more person calls me ‘ma’am’ and says ‘I’m sorry but’ I’m going to lose any control that I’m fighting to hang onto. Someone, *anyone*, tell me *right now*, what happened to my son!”

A man with a stethoscope draped around his neck took her by the arm and led her out of the waiting room into what looked to be a private office. He sat her down and was getting a cup of water from a cooler in the corner of the room as he spoke. He handed her the cup and sat on the edge of the desk in front of her.

"Mrs. Johnson, my name is Dr. Gardner, the one who will be handling your son's care while he's here in our emergency department."

"Please, please tell me what happened, Dr. Gardner."

He blew air between pursed lips and Kristen's back stiffened. "Chris was at a party tonight at the lake. Did you know that much?"

She nodded and he continued.

"According to what I've heard so far, everything was going fine until a small group of town misfits crashed the party. They were evidently angry they hadn't been invited and when they found out it was in honor of Chris, things escalated to violence. Neither Chris nor his friends started a fight, nor did they ever, at any point, touch any of the other men. It all happened so fast no one had time to react."

Kristen squeezed her hands into fists. "All *what* happened so fast? Will you please, for the love of God, tell me what is wrong with my son?"

"One of the thugs hit Chris across the back with a burning log from the bonfire ..."

"Oh God, is he burned? How bad is he?"

Dr. Gardner gently pushed her back into the chair. "No, Mrs. Johnson, Chris isn't burned. He has a long bruise across his shoulder blades but that'll heal and it's nothing to worry about."

"Then why is everyone acting as if his injury is so severe? I just don't understand!"

"When Chris was hit with the wood, he fell to his hands and knees. While he was in that position, he looked up at one of his attackers and that's when he hit Chris in the head with the blade of an ax."

Kristen stared at the doctor as if he had begun speaking in a foreign language. She started shaking her head in denial, then began to chant, "No, no, no, no, no ..."

"Mrs. Johnson, I need you to focus. I need to ask you questions. Is Chris allergic to any medications? Latex? Adhesive tape? Does he take any type of regular medication? Does he have any health issues I should know about?"

Kristen jumped up and screamed, "You mean other than an ax in his head? Nope, that'd pretty much be his only little problem at the moment! Is he dying? Will you at least tell me that much?"

"No, he's far from it, Mrs. Johnson. In fact, it's safe to say that he's shocked our entire hospital staff. Not only is he still alive—he's alert, he's breathing on his own, and he doesn't seem to be having much pain."

"What? That's impossible! Isn't it? I want to see my son right now!"

"I'll take you in there but I want to warn you, he does, in fact, have an ax sticking out of his skull. At the moment we're running tests, taking x-rays, possibly a CT scan soon. No one's removing that ax until we know exactly where it sits inside his brain, and if there's any bleeding or substantial swelling. Removing that ax before we have all the answers could kill him. I want you to understand all this before I take you in there. Chris is holding up beautifully; I need you to be as strong as he is. Chris needs for you to do that. Can you, Mrs. Johnson?"

"Absolutely. I can do anything I have to for my son."

Her teeth were chattering and she slipped her tongue between them so no one could hear it. She wiped at her tears which only caused her mascara to smear but Chris would expect her to be upset. He just didn't need her to fall apart right now.

He was sitting up at a 45 degree angle, his body still strapped to a backboard, the cervical collar still in place and a white gauze bandage wrapped around his head so thickly it looked like a turban. That image was ruined by the ax handle protruding outward from Chris' forehead. His eyes were red and his skin was pasty, but he smiled when he saw his mom.

"Baby, how are you doing?"

"Not so bad, Mom, but I've got a splitting headache." He winced when he forced a small chuckle.

"How bad is the pain, Chris?"

"You may not believe this, Mom, but it doesn't hurt that much. One of the nurses said that sometimes head trauma is a lot less painful that most people think it is. Something about the nerves and all ... oh, I don't remember what all she said. All I want to hear is someone telling me they're going to pull it out. But I'm also scared someone's going to tell me they're going to pull it out. Either way it's going to suck."

Dr. Miller came in carrying a large manila envelope. He pulled out many different x-rays, taken from every possible angle. Each time he slapped one into place on the viewing window, he shook his head in amazement. After they were all up, he turned to the mother and son and said, "I simply cannot believe this! Chris, you believe in God? I sure hope so because he sure believes in you!"

For the first time since the nightmare began, Chris began to feel a whisper of hope. Kristen grabbed his hand.

"What do you mean, Dr. Gardner? Is my son going to be alright?"

"Let me walk you through this, Mrs. Johnson. Chris, who should be, by all accounts, dead on that table, is a walking, talking miracle. When that jerk hit him with the ax, the blade sunk in only four inches. Okay, not only is the blade not too deep, it slid into the perfect placement, right smack dab in the middle. The brain has two hemispheres, with a depression between them. That's exactly where the ax went in—not deep enough to cause catastrophic injury and not enough to cause any brain damage."

Kristen's entire face was wreathed in a smile. "So, what's next?"

Chris' eyes rounded and grew large. "Yeah, what's next?"

"Next we take you to surgery and slooowly pull that blade free. We wash out the wound, double check for any further injury or bleeding, then we sew you up and take you to ICU for a couple of days just to make sure you continue to do well. Really, I don't anticipate any problems. Of course, there are risks with even the most mundane surgery and this is far from mundane, but I think God was smiling on you tonight, Chris. I don't see why he'd change his mind at this stage of the game."

"This is amazing! I have an axe imbedded in my skull, but it's going to be okay?"

The physician took the young man's hands into his. "Chris, God must have a special plan for you, son, because that is the only reason I can find for this miracle. Now, tell your mother goodnight like a good boy so I can take you to surgery." He then shook Kristen's hand. "The next time you see your boy here, Mrs. Johnson, he'll be minus the headgear. I hope you haven't grown too fond of it."

Kristen laughed and threw her arms around the doctor. "Take care of my son, Dr. Gardner. I know it'll go well because God is guiding your hands."

"I agree, Kristen. May I call you, Kristen?"

"Yes, of course, Dr. Gardner."

"Jeremy. My name is Jeremy Gardner."

Mother and son watched the surgeon walk through the doors. Chris grinned and said, "Ooh la la, I think Mom has a boyfriend."

"You're unbelievable, Chris Johnson! You sit there with an ax in your head, teasing me about something that silly! Now, give me a kiss and tell me I'm the best mother in the world, then I'll let you go to surgery."

"Really? You promise you'll let me go to surgery? Oh gee, you're just the best mother in the world!" He laughed, then moaned. "Okay, enough of that. I love you, Mom. I've got to go see a man about an ax. See you later!"

Emily, Rick, and several of Chris' other friends were waiting when Kristen sat down. She told them the amazing news. But even though all the young people were relieved, it was clear they wouldn't accept it until they saw Chris after surgery.

The two hours that the surgery took seemed to last twenty-four. During that time, the assembled group found out that all four of the party crashers had been arrested, but not without incident. Ben and Devin fought so hard to evade capture they had to be tasered and Ben broke his leg when he jumped from a high fence he'd climbed to get away from the K9 officers. They were all in custody and had confessed they were high when they'd attacked Chris. No one believed that would keep them from prison for attempted murder.

The surgery was as big a success as Dr. Gardner anticipated. In a matter of days, Chris was back home, being unnecessarily nursed by Emily and his mother, when she was home. Because of the assault, Chris decided to wait a few months to see if he still wanted to reenlist. After his experience, he felt he wanted to go for an M.D.

Those few months turned into two years in which life took all of them by surprise. It turned out there were two weddings and one new addition to the family. Kristen's thank you notes came from Dr and Mrs. Jeremy Gardner, just six months before Emily married her Chris. Therefore, it seemed only fair that Kristen have her baby first, too.

Joshua Gardner was five months old when his niece, Alana Johnson was born.

Big Things Come in Small Packages

"Mommy?"

Jessica leaned around the corner and saw her son's freckled face partway through the screen door.

"What is it, Rusty? What did you do this time?"

"I didn't do nothin', Mama. I just wanted to show you something."

"Is it something I have to come outside to see or something you're bringing in the house to show me?"

"Well, it'd be okay either way, but I'll just go ahead and bring it on in. You're goin' to like it, Mommy."

"It better not be another big old turtle, Russell James Daniels! And it better not be another poor baby bird that fell out of the nest that we have to watch die. And so help me, if it's another gerbil, hamster, rat or whatever you call them that someone's mother told him he had to get rid of so he gave it to you, it's going right back where it came from. And never again bring in a field mouse you rescued from Mrs. Talley's cat. Just no more weird animals, Rusty, and I mean it!"

"It ain't a weird animal, Mama." Rusty had come to stand so close behind her it started her when he spoke.

She turned to see his hands clasped together as if in prayer and Jessica got a bad feeling. "What is it, Rusty? What did you managed to scavenge this time?"

He opened his grimy little boy hands, complete with blisters from digging a hole for the baby bird that hadn't survived, bruises from where Mrs. Talley's cat had scratched him repeatedly, trying to retain custody of the little mouse she intended to eat as soon as the silly little redheaded boy would j-u-s-t-l-e-t-g-o, but the boy was

94

stronger and more determined. In the smallest of gaps made when Rusty opened his praying hands just a little, a tiny black nose stuck out, sniffling the air, trying to figure out the new scents.

"That better not be a raccoon, Rusty! No? What is it, then? Possums don't have black noses, do they? Okay, you know what? Just never mind. I don't care what it is, get it out of my house. No matter what you call it, it's an animal and I ain't allowing no more animals in, or around, this house. Now get! I mean it. Get it on out of here!"

There are few things in the world more heart-tugging that the crestfallen face of a five year old. No matter how bad her day had been, that adorable face that she loved more than life itself, got to her every time.

Jessica put her hand on her son's shoulder to stop him, then knelt in front of him, peering into those tiny hands. "Okay honey, what do you have there?"

Rusty was hesitant as he loosened his grip on the small creature. A brown furry head no larger than an orange popped up and began to lick at the little boy's dirty fingers. Ears stuck up like those of a doe and large brown eyes glanced nervously at the person who had been yelling just moments before.

"Oh Rusty, no. That dog is part Chihuahua and God only knows what else. Those dogs are mean, bark all the time, shake all over, and pee on the floor every time you look at them. No Rusty, absolutely not! We can't afford to have any pets but even if we could, it sure wouldn't be a Chihuahua. Now, take him back wherever you found him."

"Her."

"What? It's a girl? That's even worse. All we need is a dog having puppies."

"She's just a baby, Mommy. I'll take good care of her, I promise. I'll do all the work; you won't even know she's around. I'll fix her a bed in my room and—"

"I've already told you, Rusty, *no*. Now, take her back outside and leave her where you found her."

"But Mama—"

"Now, Rusty!"

He cuddled the tiny dog in his arms and clumsily opened the door. He stopped in the open doorway and turned to look at his mother. He lifted his eyebrows but she shook her head. He again dropped his head and went on outside, allowing the door to close softly behind him.

Jessica stepped to the window and watched Rusty as he trudged across the yard to the woods. She saw him turn back around and go into the ramshackle shed at the side of the house. Through the open doorway of the shed, she watched him pick up an old horse blanket and wrap the dog inside, then he resumed his walk into the woods.

Her heart ached for Rusty, but it was time for him to start seeing the real world and just how unfair it was. It was time he be allowed to see the secret of poverty, so he could begin to understand the reality of their life. Since her husband had left them, with no forwarding address and no money, it was up to her to keep them alive as best as she could. Her job at the steak house didn't pay much and every penny in tips was as precious as gold. For two years she'd kept the utilities on, passable food on the table, and a telephone for emergencies, as long as she made no long-distance calls. Not that she had to worry about that; she had no one to call. She'd been an only child and both parents were gone so it was just her and Rusty. There wasn't enough extra money to feed even a small dog.

She sighed deeply as she opened two packages of Ramen noodle soup. She'd give the crackers to Rusty; she didn't mind not eating the extra calories. She chuckled without humor; she was so thin now she really didn't have to worry about gaining any weight.

She had a couple pieces of bread and a slice of cheese. A grilled cheese sandwich, split between the two of them, along with the soup should be enough dinner to fill them up. She had it ready to eat when Rusty walked back in the house.

"Go wash your hands, honey; time to eat."

Without a word the little boy washed his hands and sat down at the table. He bowed his head and put his hands together. "Thank you, God, for this food to feed our bodies. Please, baby Jesus, take care of Mutt out there in the woods since I ain't allowed to. Amen."

Jessica wearily shook her head. "Rusty, I can't help it about that dog, honey. You know we're having a hard time of it. I know you don't understand but some day you will."

"But what if I give her part of my food? I don't need to eat so much. She wouldn't eat a whole lot, Mommy. See? I can give her half my cheese sandwich and ..."

"You want to give half of your half of sandwich to a dog? No, Rusty. You're already too thin now. She'll find some other family in the area that'll take her in; somebody else that can afford to feed her. What if she got sick and needed to go to the vet, Rusty? I don't have the money for that. I can't even afford to take myself to the doctor. I manage if you have to go, but I can't do that for a dog, son."

He didn't say anything else, just continued to eat slowly. Jessica finished and took her dishes into the kitchen, then began to clean up. "You about done in there, Rusty?"

"Yes ma'am, I'm done. Can I go outside for awhile?"

She came back to the table, picked up his dishes, and ran her hand over the back of his head. She again noted that he needed a haircut. "Just for a little bit. It'll be dark soon and I don't want you to go into the woods."

Rusty picked up a small red ball from the corner of the dining room floor. He bounced it a few times until his mother admonished, "Now, you know not to do that in the house, Rus. And don't go anywhere near that old rotten boat dock out there. As soon as I can find someone to do it, I'm going to have that thing ripped out before you get hurt on it."

He carried the ball outside and pulled the door behind him a little harder than usual. Jessica grinned in spite of herself. The child had her short fuse and his disappointment over the puppy was showing. As she washed the few plates and bowls she looked out the kitchen window. She frowned when she saw that the brown and white Chihuahua sprinted out of the trees when she heard Rusty close the door.

The boy bent over and nuzzled the little dog and she licked at his face. Then Jessica saw him look behind him at the house, as if seeing if she was watching him, and pulled something from his pocket. She watched him feed nearly half a grilled cheese sandwich to the hungry little dog that gobbled down the food as fast as he could hand it to her. Jessica sighed and dropped her head.

When she lifted her head up, Rusty and the dog were walking away from the house. No doubt he wanted to play with the dog without his mother seeing him. At the edge of the yard, Rusty gently pitched the ball underhanded so it didn't go very far. The puppy ran after it and dutifully brought it back to the little boy. Each time he threw it, she brought it back to him, her step playful and joyful.

Jessica stopped watching and put some water for tea on the stove. When she first heard the noise, she assumed it was the whistling tea kettle letting her know the water was boiling. Only after she removed the pot from the stove did she recognize the sound for what it was, a dog's high pitched howl. She stood there for a few seconds, trying to pinpoint the direction of the sound, trying to determine if it was the same place she'd last seen Rusty and that worthless dog.

As she got to the door she heard high-pitched barking and small nails scratching frantically for attention. She jerked the door open to find the Chihuahua yelping so hard that with each bark, all four of her feet bounced off the ground.

"Oh hush! Where's Rusty? Stop barking, you little brat!"

Still, the small dog persisted, barely taking a breath between each yip. Jessica's eyes scanned the yard, a frown growing between her eyebrows when she failed to see her son.

"Rusty! Where are you? Rusty? Answer me!"

The little dog now began to jump up on Jessica's pant leg, barking so hard she was becoming hoarse. She looked down at the animal, then decided the dog may be the way to find her son. She stepped out into the yard and the dog ran ahead a few feet then stopped, looked back, as if waiting for Jessica to follow.

She allowed the dog to lead the way, growing more impatient and worried with each step they took without her seeing her son.

"Rusty! Where are you, honey? Please, yell out so I can find you!" Each time she said this, she'd stand still to listen. And each time the persistent little dog would once again start yelping. Jessica's heart leaped in her chest when she saw where the pup was leading her.

Oh God, not that boat dock! I told him to not go anywhere near it. No, he wouldn't do that. He'd be afraid I'd get mad if he walked out on it.

"Rusty!!!"

When she got closer to the water, she realized that with the recent flooding, the rain-swollen river was so loud that even if the boy had called back to her, she couldn't have heard him.

Jessica was near the dock when she saw him. Three of the old wooden planks had crumbled beneath Rusty's weight and there he was, crying, trying to find something to grab onto, the soles of his shoes skimming the white caps of the water rushing beneath his twisting body. The one thing that held him up was the sleeve of his jacket had snagged on a nail that protruded from the rotten boards. She not only saw the blood soaking through the layers of cloth but the tear in the material grew larger as she stared at it.

The harsh voice of the Chihuahua's pleas broke through Jessica's frozen stance and she began running. Each step on the dock creaked loudly, alerting her that the whole thing was falling apart beneath her. Rusty was nearly at the end of the wooden structure, his arms dangling, his fingers brushing the water into which he had slid further. The boiling dark water now encased his knees and she could see that the little boy was growing tired. If he fell in, he'd be swept away from her forever.

Jessica grabbed the shoulders of his jacket just as the end of the old dock broke free to spiral out of sight in the swift current. Before she lost her grip, she dragged her son onto the increasingly fragile structure. Beside her, the small dog barked ferociously, as if to remind her they had to hurry, hurry, hurry!

Holding her son in her arms, Jessica stumbled back toward the riverbank, the now silent puppy close on her heels. They collapsed on the shore just as the entire dock was washed away by an especially violent whitecap.

Jessica fell onto her back and held her son close to her heart, her harsh sobs as loud as the brackish river whooshing past. Rain began to fall, yet the three of them lay on the ground—panting, thankful. When Jessica caught her breath she leaned away from Rusty to see how badly he was injured. The little boy just stared into her eyes, not speaking. The only sound was the chattering of his teeth. She gently pulled his arm free of the torn jacket that had saved his life and gasped when she saw the four inch gash that bled freely.

She placed Rusty in the backseat of the car and ran into the house just long enough to grab two blankets to wrap her son in and her purse. The little dog stood in the middle of the kitchen floor, watching her. Quickly, she put down an old butter dish filled with water.

"Little dog, if anyone ever deserved to find a home, you did today. For better or worse, you're now part of this family. Hold down the fort until I bring your little master back home."

The dog lay down next to the dish and watched her close the front door, already content to be the guardian of the house.

Jessica was amazed the ER was empty when they arrived and they didn't have to wait to be seen. It was a good thing since Rusty's arm continued to bleed freely, now soaking his already-wet pants, socks, and shoes.

The male nurse helped her undress the silent little boy, then brought blankets that had been warmed in a heating unit in the hallway. After the nurse wrapped the boy's arm in temporary gauze, he rubbed the top of Rusty's head. "Don't worry, big guy. We'll get you fixed up in no time. Mom? Anything I can get for you? Water? Coffee? The doctor will be right in."

His name badge showed his name was Jim Tyson. "Yes, Jim, I'd like a hot cup of coffee, if you have time."

Jim laughed, "Well, it's not exactly busy right now. Cup of coffee coming right up."

"Mommy, am I going to be okay?"

Jessica was a bit surprised at his voice since he'd been so quiet. "Yes, honey, you're going to be just fine. You may have to get a few stitches but that's something you can show off at school. Everybody, especially the other guys, thinks stitches are way cool."

Rusty's eyes rounded. "They do?"

"Well, of course they do! You see all those scars on Captain Jack, on the Pirate movies? Well, he's had a lot of stitches, and even the girls think he's pretty cool."

"Oh, I don't care what any stinky ol' girl thinks. But you really know the guys think cuts and stitches are cool?"

Jim walked in with her coffee as Rusty asked the last question. He handed her the cup with a smile and said, "Are kidding me? Stitches are absolutely the coolest thing ever! Yeah, all us guys make sure we let everybody see our stitches. Hey, they're like a badge of honor or something."

The conversation was interrupted by the doctor. He smiled as he shook Rusty's hand. "So tell me what happened, Mr. Daniels."

Rusty glanced at his mother beneath lowered lashes. Jessica smiled encouragingly. "It's okay, honey. I'd like to know how you wound up out there on the edge of that boat dock, myself."

"I got this dog ... well, he ain't my dog 'cause Mommy said I can't keep her but ... I found a puppy and named her Mutt 'cause that's what Mommy said she is. I was outside playing with Mutt and throwing a ball for her to go fetch. She did it every single time, too. She's so smart! Anyways, I threw it too far and it rolled out on the dock. Mutt started to go fetch it but then she just ran off the dock, back to me, and wouldn't go get that ball, didn't matter how many times I said 'Go on, girl, fetch!' She just sat there and looked at me."

The doctor nodded. "So you went to get the ball, yourself, and got stuck?"

"Yeah. I know I ain't supposed to go out there but I wanted to keep that ball for Mutt. I thought I'd just run out there real quick-like, get the ball and run back off the dock before Mommy saw me. Only thing is, when I got out there, the boards started breaking. I fell through the dock and would've went in the water but my coat got hung on a nail sticking out. That's what cut my arm really bad."

Jessica spoke up, "That old jacket is what saved his life. If it hadn't been snagged on that nail ... But no, that's not all of it. Mutt saved his life. If it hadn't been for her barking and pitching a fit for me to follow her, I never would've gotten to my son and he would have fallen in the river. That little dog saved his life."

"Does that mean I can keep her, Mommy?" Rusty's mouth lifted in a half smile, his eyes large and hopeful. He pumped his good arm like a winning athlete when his mother said, "You bet your boots you can keep that dog. Mutt is family now."

"Whoo hoo! I got a dog!"

The doctor laughed and said, "Hold onto that happy feeling because I have to give you a shot to numb your arm and it stings a little bit."

"I don't care if it hurts a lot, I'll be good. I'm so happy about my dog, nothing can hurt me."

True to his words, Rusty was a trooper and didn't cry when the needle injected the burning medication that quickly numbed his arm enough to get stitches.

As an aide was looking through a box of clothing kept just for people who need something to wear home, Jim and Jessica talked over another cup of coffee.

"You work down there at Reed's Steak House, don't you? I thought I remembered seeing you there. How long have you been working there?"

"For about two years; ever since I got a divorce."

"Oh, I'm sorry. I know that's got to be tough, being a single mom and all. I was raised by a single mom, myself. It was hard on her but she was a wonderful mother."

"I hope that my son says that about his mother some day."

"Oh, I'm certain he will. Say, uh, I hope I'm not coming on too strong but, well ... are you seeing anybody?"

Jessica grinned. "Nope, not a soul."

"Well, what do you say about going to a movie on Friday? We'll find a movie that Rusty can watch with us. Maybe grab a burger after?"

"I'll have to ask the man of the house but I'm sure he'd be happy to go out with you." He liked the way she laughed. "As long as the big, bad guard dog is fed, I'm sure she'll be okay with us leaving her alone again."

The movie and burgers turned into months of family-type excursions, some even included swimming lessons for Rusty. Mutt settled into her new life as household protector, even agreeably sharing her duties when Jim became a permanent member of the family.

The Good Samaritan

She ran to her car, slipping on the rain-slick sidewalk in front of her house. She never missed a chance to go to the movies with her sister, but tonight she wondered if she should have just stayed home. The idea of snuggling with Bob when she watched mindless TV with him and their sixteen-year-old daughter, Lindsey, was much more appealing than going out in a cold rain to see "The Help" again. She had liked the movie the first time she saw it when she'd gone with her husband, a decision she soon regretted.

"What? You went to see it without me? Aw, Katie, you promised we'd go together. So much for sisterly loyalty! Hmph!"

"Oh, knock it off, Cindy. It was 'date night' and it was either 'The Help' or a kids' movie. Sorry; I know I made a promise but there was no way I was going to watch that one. I don't mind seeing 'The Help' again. Just name the day and we'll go together."

"Great, a pity movie date with my sister. Okay, then let's go tonight."

"Tonight? C'mon, you need to give me more notice than that, Cindy! I was going to—"

"Uh huh, that's what I thought. Come on, Kate, you don't have anything to do tonight, anyway."

"But it's supposed to rain."

"So? You think you might melt or something? You aren't made out of sugar, are you?"

"Okay, okay, if it'll shut you up, I'll go tonight."

She could hear the smile in her sister's voice. "Cool beans! See ya around 6:30."

So here she was, at 6:00, running to her car through a frigid downpour, wishing she'd had the gumption to tell her sister she'd rather stay home tonight.

Oh, well, in four or five hours I'll be back home, warm and snug as a bug in a rug.

She was about five miles from home when she saw him. Though it was hard to see through the rain speckled windows, the boy looked to be about twelve years old, standing on the side of the road, one hand shoved in his jeans pocket, the other extended in a hitchhiker's stance, thumb pointing in the direction she was headed. His shoulders were hunched upward and the hoodie was pulled over his head to shield his face from the rain. He shuffled from one foot to the other in what appeared to be a vain attempt to stay warm.

Kate drove past him and stopped for a red light a block away. By the time the light turned green, guilt over leaving a cold, wet child on the side of the road won over common sense and she turned around. When she pulled beside him, the boy looked into the window, saw her, and opened the door. He was so wet that her car seat was soaked through within seconds of his climbing in.

"Why in the world are you out hitchhiking in this weather? Aren't you a bit young for this? Not that it's safe for anyone to hitch a ride, no matter how old they are, but ... where are your parents?"

His responding laughter took her by surprise. It sounded deeper than she'd thought it would. He pulled the hood from his head and shoulder-length dark hair tumbled out. He turned toward her just as they passed beneath a streetlight and she got her second surprise in the last two minutes. This was not a boy of twelve beside her. Oh, he was still young, possibly fifteen or sixteen, but much older than he first appeared to be. When he pulled the gun from his pocket, Kate understood the charade.

"Well, let me see. My mom's probably in bed with some meth head and my dad's in the wind, whereabouts unknown at this time, as they say in court. But really, lady, I think the location of my fine, upstanding parents is the last thing you should worry about right now, don't you?"

"Why are you doing this? I thought you were a kid, I felt bad about you standing in the rain, came back to give you a ride."

"See? It worked!"

"What do you want? If you want money, I don't have much, maybe a hundred dollars, but you can have it. It's in my purse."

"Sure, I want the money; of course I do. I like this car, lady. How much did this set you back? Or, I guess I should ask how much it cost your old man. Women always get men to pay for stuff like that."

"I don't know how much we gave for it but you can have it, too. Take whatever you want; just don't hurt me."

"Oh, baby, I'm going to hurt you. You better believe I'm going to hurt you—a lot."

"But why? I'm giving you whatever you want. Why would you have to hurt me?"

"Everything I want?" He wiggled his eyebrows up and down for lascivious effect.

Kate swallowed hard then turned to look him in the eyes. "Yes, everything. Whatever you want. So there's no reason to hurt me."

"I'll take whatever I want, so that's not a bargaining chip. Besides, I *want* to hurt you."

"Why would you possibly *want* to hurt someone? I don't understand!"

"Really? You really don't understand. Wow, you're sure stupid. I get off on it, lady, that's why. Even with an old broad like you. Now do you get it?"

Tears filled her eyes and Kate began to work on a plan to survive this night with at least her life.

"Go ahead; get the money. I have a few dollars in the billfold but there's a hundred folded into a side pocket."

"Hiding money from the hubby, huh? Now that's not very nice, is it?" The fact that she didn't see it coming caused the shock to be greater when he leaned over to backhand her, hard, across her face. "You should never hide money from your loving husband, you cow."

Sniffling back tears and the copper-tasting blood, Kate sputtered, "I didn't hide it from him. He told me to always keep a one-hundred-dollar bill folded somewhere in my wallet for emergencies. I don't hide anything from my husband."

"Well, ain't he just a regular knight in shining armor? So what does this knight do for a living?"

Oh God, what do I say? I don't want him to know Bob is a police officer. That might be all it takes to set him off. But if I say something like a doctor or lawyer, he might hit me again, thinking we're part of a society he obviously holds in contempt.

"What?"

That got her a tap on the top of the head with the gun in his hand. "I said, what does your old man do for a living? You know—his job?"

"He works at a steel mill on the west side of town."

"Well, he probably makes decent money for you to blow on silly crap."

"I wouldn't do that."

"Oh, shut up. Got a lot of money in the bank?"

"Some, not a lot."

"Well, whatever you got, I want. Where're your debit cards?"

"I've got one and it's the red one in a side pocket of my wallet."

"Great. Now what's the PIN?"

Kate spoke so softly he told her to speak up. "What are you doing? You nervous or think you can get by with giving me phony PINs? If I gave this to a friend of mine, told him the PIN you gave me, would he be able to use this card to get money out of an ATM?"

"Yes, he could, but you don't have to do that. I can drive you to one, either get the money out for you or sit in the car while you get it yourself."

Perhaps if he'll get out of the car to use an ATM, I can get free.

"Lady ..." he pulled her driver's license from her billfold. "Kate Simmons, you trying to pull a fast one on me? I might be young but I'm not stupid. Don't you worry how I get the money; I'll figure it out. Now drive to the corner and turn right."

"Where are we going?"

"Don't worry about it, okay? I tell you which way to turn and that's the way we go. Got it?"

"Why don't I just give you my keys and you can take yourself wherever you want to go?"

His snort was rude and frightening. "Lady ..." He shook his head in disgust. "You're not getting out of this car so shut your mouth. In fact, stop talking altogether."

Where are we? I'm not familiar with this is a part of town. Maybe he'll take me to the housing projects. There'd be a lot of people there and, if I could get free, I could start screaming and maybe someone would help me.

"Turn right at the next corner. Now take the next two rights."

This is away from the projects. This is near that new retirement center. Oh, even if I can get away, the residents here are too old and fragile to help me.

"What's your name?"

"I thought I told you to shut up. Didn't get the memo, huh?" He transferred the gun to his other hand so he could slap her with full force. "Think that will help you remember?"

He turned back to the rain-splattered windows, as if making a decision.

"No, wait. I've changed my mind. Turn back around. We're going to an ATM to get money, first. Yeah, first money, then a little fun and games." He let his eyes crawl over her and she shivered. "Oh, looking forward to it, huh? I don't blame ya; it'll be fun. Probably better than what you get at home from your old man."

"Listen, you don't have to do this. Take the car, take the money, the debit card, the credit cards, anything you can find in the car. Just let me go and I won't identify you to the cops. I'll say you had on a ski mask or something, that I couldn't see your face and, and, you were wearing gloves, yeah! That'll give you time to get the city limits and be long gone before they even know what, or who, they're looking for. All they'll know is the type of car it is. I promise you I won't—"

Even though she saw this blow coming, it hurt just as badly as the first one did. She could feel her left eye beginning to swell.

"Pull up to that ATM right over there. Get as much out of it as you can—whatever your limit is."

Kate had hoped he would have her use an ATM that was inaccessible from the car so she could take a chance and run as fast as possible, hoping to escape. No such luck. She withdrew $500.00 and pulled out again.

"Okay, we'll look for another one and make another withdrawal." The next closest ATM was two blocks away.

With one thousand dollars in his pocket, the man was feeling cockier. "Okay bitch, turn left at the next traffic signal and keep driving until I tell you to turn."

The car was as quiet as a tomb. Both occupants were planning their next move, both decidedly different in nature. One planned for violence, rape and possibly murder. The other planned for nothing but an escape.

Kate had driven roughly another three miles when he barked at her to turn left. His voice had been so loud, so startling in the silence, she jumped. From the corner of her eye she saw the young man grin. He reached over and ran his hand from her knee to her upper thigh. When he ventured close to her crotch, she grabbed his hand and threw it from her. He slammed the gun into the front of her face and she felt several teeth shatter.

But they were just teeth, right? Just dental work. She could lose the teeth, the money, the car and all its fancy technology and she wouldn't mind, as long as she escaped with her life. She also prayed he didn't rape her.

As if reading her mind, he leaned over and ran his tongue from her jaw line to the edge of her eyebrow. His fetid breath nearly gagged her but she kept a tight clamp on that reflex so as to not anger him again.

"Yeah, baby, we're going to have fun, fun, fun. Oooh, the things I'm going to do to you would cause you to have nightmares for a long, long time. But you won't be around to dream about me. Such a pity because I'm certain you'd never forget.

When he reached over and began to rip the buttons from the front of her blouse, it became real that she was never going to see her family again. She was never going to caress her husband and hear him whisper his love to her before they fell asleep. She was never going to be there to help her fourteen-year-old daughter grow into a woman.

The more the thought about this, the more skin he exposed as he ripped her clothes from her as she drove, the angrier she became. She took time to glance quickly at her attacker, saw that he had not put on a seatbelt, then she pressed her foot on the accelerator as hard and as fast as possible.

The thug was first thrown back against the seat. "Hey, what the hell are you doing? You better slow this car down this minute or I swear to you, woman, I'll kill you right here!"

"Okay, I can do that." That's when she saw a huge oak tree and she aimed the center of the car hood to hit the tree.

The man saw what she intended, but only had time to shout, "Stop!" before they crashed. He was thrown against the windshield but was pulling himself back as she fumbled with her own seatbelt. When her feet hit the ground she saw that she had missed her mark and there wasn't nearly as much damage done to the car as she'd hoped. No wonder he was still conscious.

She saw they were in a residential area, a nice part of town, but most of the houses were dark. One house was lit up and that's where she headed.

She'd only gotten a few feet when she heard a loud pop and she was knocked off her feet. She didn't hesitate to jump back up and run as fast as she could toward that house. When she got there, she pounded on the door with all the strength she could find. A woman who looked to be in her seventies opened the door, took one look at her, and slammed it shut again.

Oh, God, help me, please help me. I'm standing here on this porch and the light is shining down on me. I'm a perfect target for him if he's looking.

She couldn't believe he hadn't followed her to finish the job. She felt a throbbing begin in her forehead and she reached up to touch the spot. She pulled back a hand covered in blood and nearly fainted in terror. She renewed her efforts to get that door open. She knocked so hard she cracked a couple of the small bones in her hand.

The door opened again, this time by another woman who took one look at her and grabbed her arm, pulling her inside. This whole time the first lady was arguing, telling her to push Kate back out the door.

"We don't know who she is, Sister. This could all be a scam to get in the house just to rob and kill us!"

Kate began to sob, "I'm not part of a gang. I don't want to hurt anyone. I've been shot in the head. I just need help."

As the ladies dialed 911, Kate remembered that the man who had tried to kill her now had her home address—where her unsuspecting husband and daughter sat waiting for her to come home after the movie.

Kate pulled her cell phone from her pocket and called home.

"Bob, don't ask any questions, just do as I say, please, Honey. Grab Lindsey and leave the house immediately."

"Katie? What's wrong? What do you mean—"

Katie began to sob. "Bob, get her out of that house now. Someone will call you soon." A police officer took the phone from her hand and smiled. "Hello? Sir? I'm a police officer. Your wife's been hurt. I have no details yet but we're taking her to the hospital. You can meet us there."

His smile was kind when he spoke to her.

"The ambulance is here and I'm going to ride to the hospital with you so we can chat, if you feel up to it."

Kate nodded numbly then slipped into a coma.

* * *

Later Kate found out that she had remained in a coma for nearly a week. The bullet had transversed across both hemispheres of her brain, and while that did no permanent damage, it did cause massive swelling that took her consciousness with it. The doctor told her that she had no idea how close that bullet had come to taking her life.

The doctor was blunt. "It's only by the grace of God that you're still with us, Kate. If I were you, I think I'd tell him everyday how much I appreciated a second chance. That young man meant to send you to Heaven that day; God just wasn't ready to receive you yet."

"That young man" turned out to be a fifteen year old who had a long criminal record. True, his father had left but his mother was at work, as a nurse aide in the very hospital where Kate was taken. Kate heard that the mother sank to the floor and cried when she heard what her son had done. She sent flowers and a card to Kate's room, telling her how ashamed and sorry she was.

The boy was caught the same night, still driving Kate's car. He'd stopped long enough to pick up four of his buddies, all of whom held a can of beer when the car was pulled over. As they were being handcuffed, the police found out the other men had known about the plan to steal a car and a woman. It was to be their night's entertainment.

Obviously, that didn't go along with someone else's plan, though. Someone else had decided to hold Kate close to his heart and continue her life. After all, Lindsey needed her mother to show her how to grow into a woman.

It's a Long Way Down

"Do you have your first-aid kit in your backpack, Wendy?"

"Yes, and everything known to modern hiking women is in there. Sure you won't change your mind and go with?"

"Sorry, honey. If it wasn't for this contract being up for renewal with our biggest client ..."

"Yeah, I know; you'd be there in a New York minute. But that's one of the problems, you need to get out of New York more. Haven't you heard the song that tells us 'the rats keep winning the rat race?' Come away with me. No, not to ze Casbah, but to the craggy hills and steep inclines of mountain climbing."

"Wendy, you know I'd love to, but ..."

She smiled and shrugged. "Can't blame a girl for trying. I was just hoping, since it's going to be ten days before we see each other again, I could tempt you into running away with me. Maybe next year? Will you think about it?"

"I'll go you one better than that. When I get to the office, I'll submit a vacation request for two weeks off, this time next year. How's that?"

"Oh, Bryan, you'll do that? You really sure you want to extreme hike with me?"

He slid his arms around her slender waist. "Oh, baby, I want to extreme everything with you!"

She playfully slapped his hands, then reached up to cup his face to give him a soft kiss. "Do you have any idea how much I adore you?"

His devilish grin should have prepared her for his response. "Oh, sure. I know exactly how much you adore me. I mean, why wouldn't you?"

She bumped him with her shoulder, laughed, and walked into their bedroom to finish the last of her packing. "I'm so happy, sweetheart, that this time next year we'll be going together!"

Bryan came into the room, took her hand to lead her to the bed, motioning for her to sit down. He sat down beside her, still holding her hand. "You know how I worry every time you do this, Wendy, even though you're so experienced you should have your own television show to teach others how to hike safely. That's never going to keep me from worrying about you. Please, call me every day?"

Wendy leaned against him, enjoying the scent of his clean clothes, his shampoo, his light cologne, just simply the smell of Bryan. He could be standing amidst a hundred men and she'd still be able to trace his scent, even doubly blindfolded.

"I'll call you every day I can get a cell phone signal, okay? You know that's not always possible. But if I'm not back in ten days, send out the posse."

The smile slipped just a little as he stared into her eyes. "I'm serious, Wen. I'm genuinely worried every minute you're gone. It wouldn't concern me as much if you stayed on the well-known paths. I don't relax until you're back home, safe and sound."

She patted his leg and grinned. "The well-known paths are just that, too well known. I prefer hiking off that beaten path, walking the more rugged areas so I can enjoy nature and solitude. And what you really mean is you don't relax until I'm back in the kitchen, fixing you a sandwich and a glass of tea."

"Well ... yeah! I mean, the clothes don't wash themselves, darlin'."

With a soft growl in the back of her throat, she pushed him back onto the mattress and climbed on top of him, then lightly pounded her fists on her chest, her roar made less fierce by her laughter.

With one quick movement, Bryan reversed their positions but lost the battle to retain his superior stance due to laughing so hard. Wendy deftly pushed him onto to his side, jumped from the bed and bounced around the room, holding one arm extended in victory. Imitating the sound of a riotous crowd applauding she shouted, "As Wendy defeats her opponent in the Ultimate Fighting Championship, the crowd goes wild!"

Bryan pounced from the bed and grabbed her around the waist, pulling her onto the mattress with him. "Oh, no, sweetums, wrong program. This is a horror movie and you know the monster always gets up to grab the *weak, puny* little girl—"

"Weak? Puny? You *are* a monster! Why I oughta—"

Her words were interrupted by his kiss.

"Bryan, you're going to be late for work ..."

He placed one finger against her lips, grinned, then gathered her into his arms. "I'll tell them I had car trouble."

An hour later they lingered for a moment at Wendy's car, kissing, murmuring words that lovers whisper, then parted to begin their individual journeys.

During the long drive, Wendy listened to a couple of audio books and her favorite music CDs. Whenever she stopped for gas, or to visit a rest area, she paused long enough to call her parents, a friend or two, and Bryan. She always saved Bryan for last because they never hung up without making each other laugh and saying "I love you", even if, at times, it was said in an off-handed, casual way. Wendy was unsure of many things in this life, but the love of her husband was never one of them.

She pulled into the parking lot of the Comfort Inn sixteen hours after she had left home. She hoped the bed was comfortable because she had some serious sleeping to do. The long drive had tightened some of the muscles she'd need for hiking.

* * *

Golden pink hues streaming around the edges of the motel room curtains awoke her. She showered, ate breakfast, and was at the entrance of the trail within an hour. She made one call to Bryan before she took her first step off the trail.

"I'll talk to you later, when I camp for the night. Do ya miss me?"

"Well, no; the laundry hasn't piled up yet. Besides, I still have pizza left over from last night and you were good enough to dust and pick up before you left. So, babe, I'm okay for now. Check back with me in a few days and I'll probably be missing you by then."

She couldn't stifle her chuckle. "Yeah, me too, honey ... a lot."

"I have the cavalry on speed-dial but don't make me call them. Be safe, watch for wild animals, two and four-legged variety, and don't push yourself too hard. I hate to call out rescue just because you got tired and zigged over a rock when you should've zagged."

"Love you, Bryan."

"Oh yeah, love you, too, Wen. Have I told you lately that you're the wind beneath my wings?"

"That's better than breaking wind, I guess."

"It all depends on whether or not I've eaten something that builds gas like the Good Year blimp. If I have, the wind is definitely not beneath my wings, it's ..."

"Goodbye, honey."

"... really uncomfortable, especially after you've served that casserole thing with all the cabbage in it ..."

He heard her laughter as she broke the connection. The grin he wore lasted most of the day. Nobody else in the world could make him smile like his girl could.

The early part of the forest was quiet, serene; the proximity of civilization putting a damper on woodland creature activity. When she stopped for a late lunch, Wendy first began to hear sounds of the local citizenry.

Bird songs entertained her as she ate her sandwich. Creatures stealthily rustled through the underbrush causing her to be alert as she slowly chewed each bite of her granola bar. She was merely cautious during the foliage-filtered daylight hours; it was as darkness fell that she developed an edge to that caution. Though she brought something for protection, it was in her backpack. She wondered how quickly she could reach it, if the need arose.

She paused while setting up camp long enough to face the west, to take in the full effect of the day's end. It was one of her favorite things about hiking.

Like a scene from a movie, the rich-colored hues dazzled from golden peach to indigo blue. It made one realize the day must have been very important to rate such beauty. Soon the stars began to glow as the day pushed the last blue from the sky.

She tightened the ropes on the tent just as it seemed someone flipped a switch for lights. For a few minutes, the silence was as if a giant bell jar had been lowered to encompass the campsite. Then, as the loamy muskiness of the earth penetrated her nose, the whispered voices of the night creatures come alive. Wendy was always amazed at how Mother Nature can invade your senses without seeming to intrude. One of her favorite George Washington Carver quotes came to her during times like these. *I love to think of nature as an unlimited broadcasting station, through which God speaks to us every hour, if we will only tune in.*

She thought that she should call Bryan to wish him a goodnight before the cacophony of woodland music began and drowned out either her words or his responses.

"Babe!"

"Bryan, have you ever thought about just answering with a 'Hello?' What if it was your boss calling you and you answered with 'Babe?'"

"Hmm, I hadn't thought of that. However, it might merit me a raise. How's it going, Wonder Woman?"

"Oh, honey, it's perfect, just perfect. I wish you were here with me."

"Next year, sweetheart, I promise. I was just reading a book of famous quotes and found one that made me think of you. It's about communing with nature. It's not as deep, as lyrical, as some of your favorites, but I like it. 'Look at the

trees, look at the birds, look at the clouds, look at the stars...
and if you have eyes you will be able to see that the whole
existence is joyful. Everything is simply happy. Trees are
happy for no reason; they are not going to become prime
ministers or presidents and they are not going to become
rich and they will never have any bank balance. Look at the
flowers—for no reason. It is simply unbelievable how happy
flowers are.' Have you read that?"

"Ah, Osho. Yes, I know it well."

"I'll never be able to impress you, my little wood nymph.
You're always one step ahead of me."

"Oh, you're wrong there, Studdly Doright. You impress
me every day you love me. So, miss me now?"

"Um, I might start missing you tomorrow. I still have
clean underwear but that's dwindling fast."

"Uh-huh. Say good night, baby."

"Good night, baby."

Wendy built a fire, opened a can of beans, then could
barely eat for laughing as she remembered the conversation
she and Bryan had about "wings beneath his wings." She
then cleaned up the site, secured her tent, and slipped into
the kind of sleep you're rewarded with after a long day of
pushing your body to its limits.

The warmth of the sunrise awakened her. The fire had
died to embers but it wasn't hard to encourage a full flame
so she could make coffee.

She ate, finished her morning ablutions, then packed up
the campsite to begin her day. The last thing on her to-do
list was to call Bryan for a shot of love and laughter to begin
her arduous day.

She narrowed her eyes and wrinkled her nose when all
she got for her button pushing was pips and squeaks from
her cell phone. She held it high above her head, turned it
this way and that to get the sun's reflection off the screen,
only to see, "No service."

"Grrr! So much for hearing Sweetie pie's voice
whispering sweet nothings in my ear. I guess I'll have to try
him later, farther up the trail. And it'd probably be a good

idea to stop talking to myself, just in case there's a psych-savvy bear within hearing distance. Don't want to scare the wildlife."

With a grunt, she slung her backpack across her back, caught the left strap, and pulled it over her shoulder. Inhaling deeply, she took one more shot of lung-expanding air and began ascending.

She climbed through mid-morning snack and bypassed food and drink only stopping for lunch. It was one of those rare occurrences where the rhythm felt right and she felt strong enough to just keep climbing. It was at the summit of the craggy mountain that took her all day to climb, that it happened.

Wendy had one hand on the topmost center of the rock, her left foot already pushing her upward toward the precipice, when her left foot slipped. She threw her other hand out, and grabbed another outcropping of rock, her right foot scrambling for purchase in the dirt and pebbles that rained down to the slope below her now trembling body.

She allowed her left foot to slide downward a few precious inches at a time, hoping that she could slide down onto a small tree-covered rocky platform several feet below her. She knew that she'd probably break a leg or an arm, but that would be all, if she was lucky. She allowed herself the luxury of turning her head to further scope her surroundings, searching for an alternate plan. Just as she determined she had no other course of action, her hands lost all grasp on the ledge to which she'd been clinging.

It's remarkable how fast you can pray as you're falling. And it's amazing how quickly your mind goes immediately to ask for celestial assistance when your life is on the line.

Dear God, help me!

She slammed into the rocky plateau she's wished for with a bone-jarring bounce. Her brain didn't have time to register the three broken bones in her right leg and the dislocated left shoulder when the weight of her body carried her over the jagged edge.

Wendy threw out her arms as if she could grab something, anything, to stop her fall. She landed on her back, breaking it in four places before she became airborne again. A bolder halfway down the hill nearly stopped her descent, but all it did was crush her pelvis before she slid off and tumbled on.

The 60-foot fall resulted in further injuries. The upraised rocks ripped open her left thigh, all the way to the shattered thigh bone beneath; the humerus in both arms broke in several places; internal organs were torn and bruised; most of her ribs were cracked or crushed; and the back of her skull was fractured with spider cracks.

When her broken body came to a final rest, the prayer changed. *Sweet God, don't let me die.* It was her last thought before she passed out.

Pain, the kind few people ever survive, the kind that makes you think it might not be such a bad thing if you did die, ripped her from the fuzzy, quiet coma to which she had mercifully slipped.

Her first instinct was to jerk her head up to look at her injuries. A white, hot, screaming pain that reverberated throughout her entire body forced her head back to the packed hard dirt.

She closed her eyes to stop the spinning earth and darkening sky. She was unable to control the moan that escaped her bleeding lips. A fawn, startled by the abrupt noise, ran toward her mother grazing nearby and they both leaped away gracefully.

I've been lying here so long the deer thought I wasn't a threat, nothing more than a part of the surroundings.

Gritting her teeth against the next series of screams building inside her, Wendy tried to reach the cell phone in her pocket, anything to call for help. She endured for nearly two hours; moved an inch or two, lost consciousness, and awoke to repeat the process only to find the phone shattered when she worked it free from her pocket. Wendy cried until the blackness took over again.

Bryan called her phone again and left another message, again.

"Okay, if you're playing hard to get, I'll admit that you're really, really good at it. Yay! Good for you! Hoorah, you won! Now call me back because I don't want to play this game anymore. Alright, I know you're not playing a game; it just worries me less if I pretend that you are. Please, baby, call me the minute you can. I'm worried sick. And Wendy? I love you."

His next calls were to every friend and relative of Wendy's whom he could reach. He found a number for a friend his wife hadn't seen since high school and even called her. The desperation in his voice grew with each phone call he made. By the time he got to his mother-in-law, he was in tears.

"No, I haven't heard a word from her since last night, just before she made camp. I know, I know, I tried to talk her out of going, too. She's stubborn, you know that. Oh, God, what am I going to do? I've got to find her!"

Immediately after telling Wendy's mother he'd let her know if he found out anything, Bryan made his first phone call to the police.

"Yeah, uh hi, I, uh, need to report my wife missing. She left here, driving, to go hike in the mountains, two days ago. No, no, I talked to her last night, late, before bed ... But we can't wait another day to start looking for her! I'm telling you, this isn't like Wendy to not call me, or her mother, all day and night. I talk to her several times each day and ... Yes, send someone over to take a report! I'll do whatever I need to do to find her."

While the young, tired-looking officer wrote out the report, Bryan lost his patience.

"No, we did not have an argument. No, we have not talked about getting a divorce. Son, you'll meet few people in the world who love each other more than my wife and I do. Instead of trying to imply that she left me, why don't you focus on the fact that my wife could be anywhere in those mountains, hurt or ... dying." He covered his face with his hands and the officer waited for his sobs to subside. "Please, just find her. Please ..."

The investigation would grow to include several police departments, highway patrol, and park rangers. None of them would find the missing, critically injured young wife.

* * *

As the sun crawled over the horizon on the morning of the fourth day, Wendy admitted to herself she was going to die.

I can't believe it's going to end this way; that I'm going to die, alone, in the woods, with no one to bear witness except for the same creatures who will devour my body after I'm gone. Oh, God, please let them wait until after I'm gone.

Over the hours, she'd managed to move a few feet by moving one side of her body at a time, in minute increments. She'd traveled nearly twenty feet from the side of the cliff from which she'd fallen. Her only goal had been to reach a small stream so she might get a drink. It took her two days to maneuver her body close enough to lay her face in the water and drink hungrily. The first two times she drank, she threw up the water immediately. After that she drank more slowly, drinking a sip or two every few minutes.

Other than reaching the stream, her biggest accomplishment had been to get the backpack off and open. Using her teeth and gripping the bag with her biceps, screaming with each tug she made, she finally pulled a thermal blanket free.

It was nearly noon on the sixth day when Wendy was awakened by the sound of helicopters passing overhead. Because there were two, and they flew over several times, she knew they were probably looking for her. Struggling with all her might to lift her blanket to signal them, she sobbed in pain and frustration.

Exhausted and throbbing with pain, Wendy once again passed out.

The sun was low in the sky when she awoke. There were no more distant sounds of chopper blades whipping the air into a frenzied search for one lady in a deeply wooded forest.

I understand, God; I can tell it's my last night on earth. There's no way I can make it another day. Thank you, Lord, for being with me all these long hours. Thank you, God, for helping me reach the stream so I could drink. Please God, be with Bryan and Mom; comfort them with Your grace and love. And God, when you take me, can you do it quickly? Maybe just stop my heart all at once, so I don't have time to be scared? Thank you, God, for granting me salvation, for loving me, and for taking me home.

Wendy's head jerked at the sound of another rainstorm of pebbles cascading down the hillside. She closed her eyes, praying it wasn't an animal too hungry to wait for her to die.

"Blake! Hold up, buddy! You're going to fall off if you don't slow down! Blake!"

"Okay, okay Daddy. I stopped. I ain't going to fall off no mountain! Is this okay? Can I pee right here?"

The sound of their voices carried on the slight breeze blowing across Wendy's face. Oh, sweet, blessed sound that she first thought she imagined.

"Okay, son, that's far enough! Yeah, that's good enough right there. No closer to the edge now!"

"Daddy! Did you hear that?"

"What? I didn't hear anything."

"It sounded like maybe a hurt animal. Oh, Daddy, there it is again! Did you hear it that time?"

"Hurry it up, Blake. I don't know what it is, but I heard something, too. I want to get back to the car in case it is an animal. You have to be careful out—"

"Daddy, wait! That's not an animal. Look over there, Daddy! That's a lady laying over there by the creek!"

"Oh, come on, Blake! Why would anybody be ... Oh my God, you're right! It is a woman! Go to the car, son. Grab my cell phone. Be careful to not drop it. Go on, hurry!"

Wendy allowed her head to drop back to the ground. Her voice, unused for several days, grew so hoarse from her sobs that she could barely whisper now.

"Thank you, God, oh, thank you!"

Rescue crews brought equipment including floodlights so they could work into the night to bring Wendy out of the ravine. It took several attempts for the rescuers to get her phone number because she kept losing consciousness. When someone called Bryan and told him they'd found her, she heard him weeping through the phone line. When the phone was placed to her ear, all she could manage to rasp out was, "Love you."

Her post-operative coma lasted two days. When she opened her eyes it was to find a room filled with flowers, a television playing but the sound muted, her mother dozing in a recliner across the room, and Bryan with his head leaning against the bedrail. He'd tried to keep his sobs silent but his fear of losing her, his anger at his own helplessness, and his joy of having her saved, increased the volume of his cries.

When he saw her eyes were open and the smile that reached them, he leaned over her, careful to avoid all the tubes, the needles, and the machines. With tears in his eyes, he whispered, "Oh, thank you, honey, for not leaving me. I don't know what I would've done without you."

Wendy smiled through her own tears and kissed his lips. "So you're admitting that you missed me?"

With a gentle touch, he caressed her face and brushed her hair from her face. "Oh, yeah; that laundry's really piling up in the corner of the bedroom!"

The Pain of Betrayal

"Aw c'mon, Sam, that's a girlie movie. I don't wanna watch that! Dad!"

Ted's grin was already in place when he walked into the living room.

"Okay, what is it this time, my two young warriors?"

Samantha, predictably, rolled her eyes. Jacob the Informer, saw all, knew all.

"Dad, Sam rolled her eyes at you again!"

A pillow sailed across the room and landed with such precision it nearly knocked Jacob off his feet. Samantha chortled at her little brother's expression of shocked disbelief.

"Dad, did you see what she just did? She threw a pillow and ..."

He was knocked off-balance by a pillow thrown from the other side of the room. Ted was laughing so hard he didn't see the corduroy missile that was launched into his shoulder. When he saw that it was his wife, Kathy, who had hit him, he ran toward her. Her mock screams were the stuff for which extreme stuffed-cushion battles were created.

Ted started stockpiling every shaped pillow he could find. He braced himself in a corner, held up a fist and declared, "Pillow Fight Friday Night has begun!"

In the following melee, a couple of lamps were shoved off their tables, the coffee table was wiped clean of the magazines that had been bothering no one, the dog and cat hid beneath furniture far enough to avoid being hit, but close enough to watch the males of the species rule victorious. Actually, the war ended when one of the pillows popped its seams and the stuffing flew around the room, coating everything in enough feathers to make it look like a chicken ranch.

All the participants were breathing heavily but their broad grins slipped a notch when Kathy's mom voice said decisively, "Okay, I'll concede the battle, but not the war. As the winners, boys, you can clean up the mess."

"But Mom!"

"Oh, chill out, Jake! Samantha and I are going to put away the dishes and then we'll get the popcorn, fire up the ol' DVD player and argue over what movie to watch." Over the kids' heads she looked at her husband who interpreted it correctly.

"Jacob, go ahead and start cleaning. I'll be back in a minute. I need to talk to your sister and mom for a minute."

"Dad, that's so unfair! Oh, okay. I'll start but I can't do it all by myself."

"No problem, buddy. I'll be back in a few minutes to help."

It was Sam's turn to groan. "Is this about that history test? I swear to you, I studied hard but ..."

Kathy put her arm around her daughter's shoulders. "What test? No, it's not about that but maybe we should talk about your grades next."

She glanced at her dad's face, then back to her mother. "It's about Charlie, isn't it?"

They sat at the kitchen table with each parent scooting close, as if to protect her, as well as prove how important this conversation would be.

Kathy looked at Ted and he spoke first.

"Sam, we don't think Charlie is good for you. He's everything that you're not and we believe he'll eventually be a bad influence or worse, he'll do something to harm you in some way. Oh, we don't necessarily mean physically, though your mom and I disagree on the potential for that, but perhaps emotionally."

Kathy took her daughter's hand. "Honey, you don't even act like yourself anymore. Since you started dating Charlie you've stopped smiling, you're withdrawn from your friends, and then there are those grades you, yourself, just mentioned. Anytime a relationship changes you, alters your life in unhealthy ways, it's probably a good idea to break free."

Looking back and forth between them, Samantha began to cry. "Did he do something I don't know about?"

Ted sighed. "Okay, I'll start. The first time I met him, he didn't exactly make a good impression. You invited him over for dinner and we were willing to be open-minded. I came home from work and he's sitting there in my recliner."

"You got mad at him for sitting in your chair, Daddy?" Ted didn't like the tightness around her lips.

"No, let me finish, Sam. I walked in and he just sat there, staring at me. I said, 'Are you Charlie?' He said, 'Yeah. And you are ...?' I said, 'My name's Ted, and that's my chair. Do you always just sit there when someone comes in like this?' He said, 'Yeah. What about it?' I told him 'Not in this house. Here you stand up and speak to someone when they come in.' That was very rude, Sam."

"And because his manners don't measure up to yours, you don't like him?"

It was Kathy's turn to sigh deeply. "No, Sam, of course that's not all that bothers us. When you were over at your Aunt Katrina's last week you were on Facebook. You didn't log out before you left so, Aunt Kat being Aunt Kat ..."

Samantha frowned and crossed her arms over her chest. "She stuck her nose in my business!"

"Watch the attitude, Sam. She looked at Charlie's page, yes. What she saw upset her so she called me. She's not only my sister, Sam, she's your aunt and she loves you."

"Okay, Mom. What did she find?"

"She found lots and lots of pictures that would upset anyone. Some were cartoons he'd drawn, depicting violence so horrific I'm surprised someone hasn't reported him yet. There were several of him with a bottle of booze in his hand, obviously drunk, and a couple pictures of him brandishing a machete."

The young girl dropped her head, staring at her hands clasped in her lap. "Yeah, those have always bothered me, too. I asked him to take them down."

Ted rubbed his hand over his face. "Sweetheart, taking photos off Facebook doesn't change his character. Anyone that does those things isn't right for you."

She nodded, then looked at her father. "You're right, Dad. I've been thinking that maybe we're not meant to be together, that we're too different, but he keeps telling me how much he loves me."

The resolve on Kathy's face surprised her daughter. "Well, maybe this will help you decide. After you left Kat's house, Charlie and a friend of his kept posting things on his wall. Charlie said 'Hey dude, you should come over later. Sam's going to be here. We'll get wasted and crazy.' His friend said, 'Oh, we gonna sex it up tonight!' That was on his wall, Samantha, for everyone to see! It's why you're not out with him tonight; it's why I said you had to stay home."

She dropped her head into her hands, her long blond hair covering her face as she sobbed. It was hard to understand her but what Ted and Kathy heard was music to their ears.

"I'm going to call him and break up with him right now! I am so embarrassed I could just die! I'm sorry Mom, Dad. Nothing's happened like that and I'm now happier than ever that it hasn't, and it never will. Don't you worry about Charlie, you won't be seeing him ever again!"

With that she jumped up from the table, pulled her cell phone from her pocket, and walked out as she dialed her soon-to-be ex-boyfriend. Ted and Kathy hugged each other.

"That actually went better than I imagined it would, Ted. I figured she'd put up a bigger fight."

"I think it was the comments he made where everyone could read them, especially her family, that did it. Sam's a good kid. She wouldn't want her family to read that junk."

Both of them were a bit surprised when Sam came back into the room and her tears were gone. "Okay, who's fixing the popcorn? Did we ever decide which movie we were going to watch? Please don't make me watch something dorky like 'The Green Hornet'. I know Jake is thirteen and likes stupid movies like that but can we watch something like, oh, I don't know, that movie I rented today called 'Red Riding Hood?'"

Kathy started the microwave and Ted leaned close to Sam, glaring into her eyes, "Grandma, what big teeth you have!"

Sam touched her nose to her father's. "All the better to eat you with, my dear!"

Jacob groaned from the doorway. "Oh man, we're going to watch that?"

Ted said, "It would seem so, old man."

Samantha began to smile, to laugh, to act like her old self. She acted as if a heavy weight had been lifted from her shoulders. The atmosphere in the entire family had circled back to normal.

* * *

That night Ted and Kathy slept the sleep of the contented, secure in their love of family, already looking forward to church the next morning. They never heard unfamiliar footsteps in their home, or knew of the hatred that walked into their lives, until it was too late to stop it.

It was loud, harsh, painful gunfire in their bedroom that woke Ted. He reacted in instinct.

He threw his arm up to shield himself, yet he took several rounds up the arm, the shoulder and finally, a blast to the face. That is the shot that threw him out of bed. While lying there, he could hear himself gurgling but he couldn't feel the blood coming out of his ears, his nose, his jaw. He couldn't feel his body. He didn't yet know it, but he was shot eleven times.

Ted kept slipping in and out of consciousness. Whenever he awoke, he kept thinking about his children upstairs, sleeping, unaware. Before he passed out again, someone walked over to where he lay face down and kicked him in the foot; yet Ted forced himself to be silent. The only sound he heard was heavy breathing and the reloading of the gun. Unable to move, he lay there anticipating the person shooting him in the back of the head.

I know that this time it's all over. All I ask, God, is make it quick.

For a few minutes, the gunman just sat on the side of the bed, breathing heavily, then stood and walked away. Because they left a small light burning in the kitchen that illuminated the hall through the open bedroom door, Ted had seen the shooter's face but he was too injured to think, to reason, who it was. Ted's addled mind thought it was a home invasion robbery.

He heard footsteps climbing heavily up the stairs, and then he heard his youngest son, Jacob, yell out, "No! Don't! Why you doing this, Charlie? Please don't hurt us, Charlie!"

That's when the gunfire resumed. At that point, due to pain and loss of blood, Ted's head dropped to the floor and he lost consciousness again. That's why he never smelled the gasoline, or knew that Charlie and his accomplice had set fire to the house.

When Ted awoke again, he saw the room filled with smoke. He turned his head to see through his open bedroom door that the fire was in the hallway close to the stairs leading to the kids' bedrooms. He began to panic but the adrenalin gave him the strength to stand. He took a step toward the bedroom door and that's when he realized he couldn't reach his children that way.

He fell back down then crawled to the other side of the bedroom. There he found Kathy, his wife, his partner, his love, his mate of eighteen years. There was no need to even check for a pulse. Charlie had sliced Kathy's throat with that same machete she had seen in the photograph. She was so butchered, her body was so horrific, Ted knew there had been no way for her to survive her murderer. The amount of blood splattered proved she'd fought as long, as hard, as she could before her life drained from her body.

Terry's next thought was again of the children. The adjoining bathroom had a door that gave access to the laundry room that, in turn, opened into the kitchen. When he saw flames licking the walls and heard the ceiling beginning to cave in, and windows exploding in the living room, he realized he couldn't go that way, either.

He stepped back into his own bathroom that was now filled with smoke. Even though he'd lived in that house for years, had been in that bathroom every day of those years, the smoke disoriented him to the point that he got lost. He kept thinking there was a window in the room, but he didn't know where it was.

He was hot, panicked, bleeding profusely, and fighting to stay alert. He moved until he found a wall, then just shuffled his feet, moving sideways, until he found the one window in the room. When he reached it, he couldn't open the window. He began to beat on it, hoping it would break and he could open it that way, but it was solid, unbreakable.

God, help!

At last, with what seemed to be his last ounce of energy, Ted shoved one more time and the widow shot upward. He knocked the screen from the window and stuck out his head. After choking on blood and smoke, that first gasp of fresh air felt sweet and pure. But he felt and heard that the house was literally caving in on him so he crawled onto the roof. There was a four or five foot drop. It was such a mind-jarring jolt to his badly injured body, that it took his breath away. He shook it off.

I've got to get to my kids.

He made his way around the side of the house only to find flames were shooting out all the windows.

Oh, God, the house is coming down!

He looked over at his neighbors' house, four hundred yards away and it might as well have been miles. He knew he had to reach that house where its residents were blissfully ignorant of the terror happening next door.

There were no stars, even the moon was hiding, as Ted began his trek. He crawled a few steps, managed to stand, stumbled a few more steps before falling back down to begin crawling again. He crawled on his belly, crawled on his hands and knees, getting cut by thorns and tree roots, but continued to push himself to keep going, no matter what. *Please God help me make it to the only people who can help.*

He made it about halfway and stopped to lean against a tree. He looked back at his home, now completely engulfed by fire and realized it was over, there was no hope of rescuing his family. No one could save them now.

No more. Please, no more. Come on, God, take me now. I don't want to live without them. He drew in as deep a breath as possible and screamed, "Enough!"

Then he became angry, and many emotions began to well up inside him. *If I die now, no one will ever know who did this.*

Ted pulled himself back to a standing position, about to turn toward the house next door when he saw movement in his own backyard. His eyes widened as he saw three people, and he struggled to figure out who they were.

As God as my witness, if it's Charlie I'll kill him. Lord, I'll kill him with my own two hands for what he's done to my family!

He took a step toward the figures silhouetted against the backdrop of sizzling fire, then fell. Using his one good arm, Ted dragged himself back to the scene of horror, noticing one of the figures runs away. As he moved closer, he realized one of them was his son. The other one was the monster who had destroyed them. Charlie was conscious but he was merely lying on his back, eyes staring at the sky, as if to count the stars shining there. Jacob stood there, huffing for breath, his shoulders drooped, and in one hand was the rifle his grandfather had given him last Christmas, the gift that had caused such arguments between Kathy and her father-in-law. The discord came to an abrupt end when Jake had told them that he appreciated the gift but there was no way he'd ever fire the weapon. He didn't want to hunt, target practice didn't interest him, and he could never fathom a reason to shoot at another human being. Until tonight.

"Jake, you okay, son? Where's Sam? Did she get out?"

Jake saw all; knew all.

It wasn't fair that so much heartbreak should be reflected in the eyes of one so young.

"Of course she got out, Dad. She got out before her boyfriend started killing us."

"Wha ...? What do you mean, Jake? Did she hear a noise and run? I don't understand."

Both of them turned toward the sound of frantic running in their direction. Samantha stopped a few feet away, taking in the scene of her home collapsing in a fiery desecration, her bloodied father and brother, and Charlie lying, unmoving, on the ground. Ted tried to lift his arm to her.

"Oh, baby! You're safe! How did you ...?"

Rushing past them, Samantha fell to her knees beside the prone body of a murderer.

"Charlie? Oh honey, wake up! Come on, baby, don't leave me! I love you, Charlie. Do you hear me?" With the anguished scream of one who has truly lost all she cared for, came the words, "Charlie, I love you!"

Jacob held his father's gaze, then dropped his head as tears ran down his bloodied, dirty cheeks. His legs covered with cuts he had endured jumping through a window, finally gave way and he sank to the ground.

The sirens grew louder in the distance, but Ted could scarcely hear them over the breaking of his heart.

Charlie's male accomplice was never found but his female partner in crime, Samantha Rene Allison, was charged as an adult and sentenced to life in prison. Throughout the entire ordeal, the only tears she had shed were for the death of her lover. Her father would cry for the rest of his life.

During the trial it came out there was only one reason Jacob was still alive. He never heard the gunshots that nearly killed his father, or the attack that took his mother's life. He had been sleeping deeply when he had a dream. In the dream a voice had told him to get the rifle he'd packed away in a box beneath his bed. The dreaming Jake had shaken his head in denial, and told the voice that he hated that gun, all guns. He turned away but the power of the voice forced him to listen.

Get out of the bed. Get the gun. NOW.

Feeling silly, Jacob climbed out of bed and had just loaded the rifle when Charlie kicked open his bedroom door, with a gun pointed right at him. Jacob yelled at the young man they'd welcomed into their home, shared a meal with, even watched movies with. Gentle Jake had been forced to fire his own weapon as Charlie shot at him, blessedly missing him every time. He obeyed blind faith and allowed the weight of his body to take him through the window next to his bed.

A mortally wounded Charlie had followed him through the window. Whether it was to finish the job, or to escape the fire, no one would ever know.

Jacob destroyed the rifle after the trial and moved with his father into his Aunt Katrina's home until they could find a new one.

He grew into a serious, studious young man who now tours the country speaking about watching for the subtle signs of impending violence, especially in teenagers. He met a nice girl in college and gave her a ring for Christmas.

"Dad, want to be my best man? You can even bring that pretty lady you've been seeing the last few months."

"Well, I'd be honored, Jake. But are you sure you don't want someone else to stand beside you as best man?"

"Dad, you've always stood beside me and you're the best man I've ever known."

It's Not Your Time

Zachary and his wife, Vanessa, had been married for five years when they decided to move from their life-long home in Knoxville to a town in Alabama. Zach enjoyed singing gospel music and had auditioned for an up and coming gospel group, hoping they would take a chance on him to be their lead. He was thrilled the day he received the call and asked his wife how she felt about moving. Vanessa loved and believed in him with all her heart and vowed to do anything for her love to realize his dream.

They did their dreaming on the sidelines. Zach went to the studios at nights and on the weekends, doing whatever it took to finish the group's new album.

Though they were dedicated workers in their "day jobs," and they both liked their jobs, there was cause for concern. The young couple had jobs as home health nurses, trained RNs working in homes all over the city. But it seemed most of Vanessa's clients were in the territory of town well known for gang wars. To offer protection, Zach was there, every night, to pick her up at work.

One night Vanessa had a feeling that came over her and no matter how hard she tried, she couldn't shake it off.

I just know something bad is about to happen. I don't know what it is, Lord, but please watch over Zach and me.

Just as she whispered those words, Zach pulled his car in front of the house where she was working. She heaved a sigh of relief and began preparations to leave.

Before Zach could get out of his car, he heard bullets ringing out. He ducked down into his seat, trying to quickly glance around, to find the source of the shooting. He heard a sharp ping as a bullet rang off his radiator. That's when he heard two more bullets hit his driver-side door in rapid succession. He decided to hit the gas and get off that street as fast as possible. He heard a few more shots as he turned the corner, then no more, but he kept on rolling.

However, he wasn't able to drive very far because steam was pouring out of his radiator. He had to pull over. When he got out of the car, he saw the tires on the driver's side were both flat and there large-bore holes in the rocker panel. As steam covered him like fog, he remembered.

Oh, my God—Vanessa! I hope you stayed inside that house, baby.

Their routine had always been that the minute Zach pulled in front of the facility, Vanessa would walk out and get in the car. That way neither one was out in the open, in that part of town, for a long length of time. But Vanessa was not only a smart woman, she'd been having that sick sense of something bad all day. So she had not immediately stepped outside this time when her husband pulled up. Even though she thought she was only hearing fire crackers being shot off, she felt that God was holding her inside. Vanessa was a true child of God and made it a point to never argue with Him.

She watched Zach pull his car away from the front very quickly so she stood there, inside, waiting ... and praying. A few minutes later she heard a rapid knock on the front door and she opened it when she saw her husband. Even though she was yet to know what had happened, she threw her arms around his neck.

"Zach, are you alright? All day I've have such a bad feeling ..."

"No, baby, I'm not. Somebody just shot at me. They messed up the car and scared me half to death. I need to call the police."

His hand was shaking a bit when he picked up the phone and dialed 911.

"... Yes sir, this is a bad area and I'm sure there is gang activity here but this is where my wife is working ... What?

Oh, dear Lord. Yes, yes, I hear you. Okay, I will. Please hurry."

Vanessa's lovely face was creased with deep lines, her eyes round and filling with tears in anticipation of bad news. "What is it, Zach?"

"The officer said that young kids around here want to join the gangs. Their lives are hard, they're hungry, their parents are meth addicts or hookers ... in other words, they want to belong to something, to someone. They think even being part of a gang is better than nothing."

Tears spilled over Vanessa's cheeks, tracking mascara in its wake. "Oh, honey, that's so sad. I can't imagine a life so terrible I'd trade it for being part of a gang. That's one thing our kids won't consider. Yeah, that's terribly, terribly sad."

"Well, babe, it's not sad enough to die for. Their initiation rite is to shoot innocent people to prove their devotion. I was nearly one of them, just now."

She rushed to his side, putting her arms around him and held him in a tight embrace. "Oh, honey, what should we do now?"

"The cops just told me to go stand by my Jeep and they'll send a car over."

"Zach? That can't be a good idea, honey. I mean, you've been shot at already and they told you to go back to your car?"

"Hey, there they are now, 'Nessa. Stay here. I'll go talk to them and come back as soon as I can."

Zach met the officers by his jeep. As they talked, the officers looked over the numerous holes in the car body.

"Man, I can't believe somebody shot at me! Look at my Jeep! Aw, man, this jeep is my baby!"

"Stay here, Mr. Hill. The tow truck should be here soon. We're going to go shake a few doors, try to rustle up a few gang bangers."

Nervously, Zach paced back and forth next to his vehicle. It didn't take long for his patience to wear thin so he walked a few more feet down the sidewalk to look for the tow truck.

That was when everything began to spiral into chaos. Zach heard bullets ring out behind him. He turned to run because the bullets were coming past him.

The first bullet hit his left thigh area and went straight through. He tried to run as fast as he could but was again shot through the left thigh. As he was crumpling to the ground, a fourth shot went completely through his leg. Lying on the ground, he was astounded when another bullet hit the ground then ricocheted up in that very same thigh.

He lay there, filled with shock.

I cannot believe I just got shot-five times!

He was shot five times but with the exit wounds, he had ten bullet holes in one leg. One had nicked his femoral artery, a grievous wound that could cause him to bleed to death within minutes.

Unable to stop himself, knowing it could mean the end of him, Zach turned toward the direction of the gunshots. There, partially hidden by a large tree, stood a mere boy, appearing to be no older than ten years old.

No, that's just not possible. I couldn't have just been shot by a kid! Why, he's no older than my youngest brother. I must be losing my mind.

"Hey you, kid! Yeah, you! I see you trying to hide behind that tree. What's wrong with you?"

The child didn't answer, just stood there with his arm extended, gun in his hand and finger on the trigger.

Zach struggled to stand, at last gaining his feet by pulling himself up by holding onto a lamppost. He knew he had to find help, quickly

With his mouth drawn in a tight line, he began limp straight toward the boy and his gun. The child didn't blink.

"In the name of Jesus you are not going to shoot me again. The power of God forbids it. I trust in my Savior, young man. Who do you trust in? You trust those older boys, who you admire so much, are going to save you? If you were shot, if you were dying, do you believe any of them would be with you?"

The hand holding the gun began to waver, shake as if palsied, and the young boy started to lower his arm.

Though his voice was rapidly growing weaker, and the tone was far from being record-quality, Zach felt led to sing one of his favorite gospel songs.

♪ Oh oh Lord, I want you to help me. Oooh Lord, I want you to help me. Help me on my journey, help me on my way. Ooooh Lord, I want you to help me. ♪

Zach was within ten feet of the boy when he saw the tears sliding down the child's face. The arm slowly fell to his side, the gun clattering to the ground. The boy took a step toward the man he'd shot, then stopped, doubt and fear showing.

"Son, please help me."

Zach fell to the ground and heard the sounds of the boy running away. With each beat of his heart, he felt more and more blood pump from his body. He grew colder than he'd ever felt before in his life. He knew, no matter if the boy chose to help him, it would be too late.

When I woke up this morning, God, I didn't think this would be the day I'd die, but I'm ready. Please watch over my Vanessa, Lord. Hold her in your loving arms and keep her safe. And God, please don't let my death be in vain. Enter that little boy's heart, imprint the image of my death there, and help guide him to a better life.

Zach slipped into darkness, never hearing the emergency crews arriving to help him.

Even unconscious, Zach slowly became aware of a lightening in his body, as if all the weight of his physical being was being taken away. He had a sensation of floating, of being surrounded by white, billowy clouds, and the loss of every concern he'd ever had in his life.

He felt his own lips lift in a wide smile at the feeling of peace and joy that filled him. If it had been a physical sensation, he would have said he felt better than he could remember in a long time.

Zach never heard Vanessa's scream, or the way she sobbed his name, begging him to stay with her. He never felt the needles the paramedics inserted into his veins. He never felt the ambu mask pressed tightly to his face or the forceful blows to his sternum as they did chest compressions. He never heard them tell his wife that he had less than a five percent chance of surviving.

As Vanessa cried, she prayed, as Zach was nearing the doorway to Paradise.

He felt a love that few living mortals have ever known. In fact, unless they've been next to the throne of God, they've never felt what was in Zach's heart at that moment.

* * *

When the paramedics relinquished possession of Zach, the doctor discovered Zach had lost over fifty percent of his body's blood.

"Call the blood bank and tell them we need all the O negative they have available. STAT!"

Zach heard none of that. What he heard, instead, were people talking, children laughing, and singing. He saw colors he'd never seen before, glowing iridescently throughout the clouds. It felt as if his chest would explode with joy.

Oh yes! This is where I'm meant to be. This is home and it's so good, Lord, to finally be home.

He felt as if he had stepped forward but then he ran into some type of invisible barrier. No matter how hard he pushed, the barrier remained intact, unyielding, unbreakable. Suddenly he heard a voice. The words he heard were impossible to accept.

"No, Zach. It's not yet your time. This is not the day you come home. You must go back."

Zach became angry and shouted, "No! I don't want to go back to a life of pain and misery. A place where young children will pick up a gun and kill you! It hurts there! It's torture on earth. I died. I gave up that life. This is where I want to stay. Please don't make me go back!"

Once more, he heard the words, "No, Zach. It's not your time. I love you and I'll be here when you come back; when it *is* your time."

Zach cried and pleaded, "Please, no. Don't make me go back to that cruel world! Please let me stay." But Zach felt himself slipping backward. The further and deeper he went, the heavier his body felt. As the surgeons shocked him for the fifth time, Zach's spirit was reunited with his pain-filled body.

He opened his eyes. The doctor holding the paddles gasped, then smiled and said, "Welcome back, Zach. You sure made us work for that one!"

Because there was a tube in Zach's throat to maintain an airway connecting him to a ventilator, he couldn't speak, but he felt utter devastation.

Vanessa was there the day they removed the tube. She hugged him after he was extubated. Her face was wreathed in smiles and her entire demeanor illustrated how happy she was to have her husband back.

For the next week Zach spoke only when spoken to. His only activity was to stare at the ceiling with a deep frown on his face. Then Vanessa came bearing gifts and a tongue-lashing.

"What is wrong with you, Zach? You survived, yet you seem sorry that you did. You're not living. You're only existing, as if you're simply waiting for death, like you're sorry you lived. You were more alive when the machines were keeping your body functioning. Well, that's enough!"

She threw a gift box onto his bed, then followed it with a large floral-decorated satchel of some sort.

Zach picked up the brightly colored bag and glared at his wife. "What's this ugly purse-thing? It looks like a ..." His eyes grew large and he stared at Vanessa with growing understanding.

"It's the reason you're still alive, Zach, that's what it is! That 'ugly-purse thing' is representing new purpose for your life. Go ahead, open the other one." Tears were streaming down her lovely face.

Zach tore open the gift box to find a small package of diapers and a receiving blanket. He raised his brimming eyes to look at his wife and held out his arms.

Vanessa rushed to his side. "Yes, that's right. Your new purpose in life is being a father to this baby. You're going to teach him, or her, how to grow into a kind, loving, determined adult, just like Daddy. You're going to not only take this baby to church, but you'll be able to relate just what waits for us on the other side. You're going to help guide the newest arrival from Heaven into a life of love that only you and I can give. That, Zach, is now your purpose."

"It's going to take me a lifetime to be able to explain just how beautiful this life, and the next one, is going to be. Got any names picked out yet?"

More from Gloria Teague

- *Beyond the Surgeon's Touch: One Miracle Away from Death*
- *Saturday Night Cocoa Fudge*

Available online from your favorite bookstore.

CPSIA information can be obtained at www.ICGtesting.com
Printed in the USA
BVOW010406190613

323699BV00013B/237/P